TRACKING THE TORCHBEARER

Poems

By

R. N. Taber

Colour, creed, sex, sexuality...these are but part of a whole; it
is the whole that counts.

First published in Great Britain in 2012 by Assembly Books, C-Hammond House, 45a Gaisford Street, London NW5 2EB.

ISBN 978-0-9539833-7-7

Printed by: http://direct-pod.com

Front cover image: www.dreamstime.com
Overall cover design; G. J. Collett

Also by the author:

Poetry:

Love and Human Remains ©2001
First Person Plural ©2002
The Third Eye ©2004
A Feeling for the Quickness of Time ©2005
Accomplices to Illusion ©2007
On The Battlefields of Love ©2010

Fiction: Laurence Fisher (trilogy) Books 1 & 2
Blasphemy ©2006
Sacrilege ©2008
                                        Also

Catching Up With Murder ©2011

ACKNOWLEDGEMENTS

I would like to thank all those editors and publishers who have included my work in various poetry magazines and anthologies world-wide since I first began submitting poems for publication in 1993. Many thanks also to friends and readers who have continued to encourage me on-line as well as off-line since I bought my first computer in 1997. A special thank you has to go to my close friend Graham Collett who has listened to me reading many of my poems; he also designed the covers for *Accomplices To Illusion* and *On The Battlefields Of Love* as well as taking responsibility for the cover of this collection.

INTRODUCTION BY THE POET

Here in the UK this year, we are celebrating the Olympic Games coming to London and Her Majesty the Queen's Diamond Jubilee. On a more personal note, I am celebrating my twentieth year of getting poetry into print.

I first began submitting poems for publication in 1993, since when some 600+ poems have appeared in various poetry publications world-wide (excluding any that only appear in my collections); if I include titles that have appeared in more than one publication, the total rises to 650+. Needless to say, I thrilled; it's not a bad tally for someone a work colleague once wryly described as 'a nobody with literary pretensions' simply because I get very little media attention. [Do I care?]

Some readers may judge that a disproportionate number of villanelles and kennings appear in this volume. I will usually choose the villanelle form to record significant national and world events; also places I have visited where, instead of a camera, I record my impressions in a poem. My kennings give expression to a more philosophical bent. Rightly or wrongly, I feel that the discipline 'form' poetry imposes on the poet summons a less blurred picture to mind, and prevents emotive waffle. Purists are welcome to take issue with my frequent use of 'hidden' rhyme.

Some of my critics argue that rhyme and form constitutes 'old hat' poetry. Yet, if variety is the spice of life, the same goes for poetry surely? Besides, readers seem to like it and it's you, the reader, not the critic who really matters.

Why do I write poetry? Well, because I enjoy it and because it helps me focus on surviving the various slings and arrows of everyday life. As someone prone to bouts of depression, I fear I would otherwise lose the plot altogether. It is also very gratifying to receive feedback, positive or otherwise. Many UK public libraries stock some or even all my titles while the number of readers world-wide who dip into my poetry blogs from time to time continues to rise significantly.

As a librarian all my professional life, I am thrilled that the British Library has decided to include my poetry blogs in a project archiving certain websites. This, in addition to my poetry reading on the 4th plinth in Trafalgar Square for Antony Gormley's *One & Other* 'live sculpture' project; the entire web stream of 2,400 people doing their own thing for one hour 24/7 over 100 days July-October 2009 is now archived in the British Library.

Another new project has been uploading readings of some of my poems to You Tube with my close friend Graham Collett acting as cameraman; he also edits all our videos before we upload them. He is also responsible for production and/or design of some of my book covers, including this one. It has been great fun, and if results are not always ideal, we hope readers will enjoy what is very much a team effort. While we have done our best, we haven't taken it too seriously, not least because any art form, including poetry should, above all else, entertain. (I fear critics are frequently inclined to overlook this essential feature of the arts.)

While my gay-interest poems have met with some hostility, most feedback has been very positive, so much so that by the time I came to publish *On the Battlefields of Love* in 2010, I felt that few readers would disapprove of my including even more gay material. *Tracking The Torchbearer*, like *On The Battlefields Of Love*, not only has a central gay section but also includes gay-interest material in other sections. [Regular readers of my blogs will know I do not consider poetry on a gay theme as something separate from mainstream poetry, nor a genre-within-a genre as some critics would have it.]

Why was I cautious, even defensive in earlier collections? Well, contrary to general opinion, gay material is (still) not seen as a good commercial proposition by most editors and publishers. I think it is significant that few poems of mine on a gay theme have been published outside my collections.

I get so fed up with hearing that 'gays have never had it so good.' This may well be true in some parts of the western world but not all, especially where multiculturalism continues to impose certain historical restrictions and taboos; among these, same sex relationships. In some parts of the world, of course, gay people, can be imprisoned, even executed for their sexuality. In Uganda, for example, in 2010, a newspaper article published the names of known homosexuals and called for them to be hanged!

It is high time the world's pockets of socio-cultural-religious bigotry came into the 21st century and got real.

Like it or not, gay people exist worldwide and should be accorded the same courtesies and Human Rights as any other responsible members of society. It may be true that much of the northern hemisphere has pro-gay legislation and political correctness, but many people simply pay lip service to these; the latter especially has much to answer for in merely driving homophobia underground.

The public face of Equal Rights often masks the private face of an enduring socio-cultural-religious bigotry.

Of course, our sexuality is only a part of who we are. Sexual identity is important, but isn't and shouldn't be the last word in life, love and human relationships. I tackle a variety of themes and events that matter to the world today. Yes, from a personal perspective, but while trying to give the reader space to move within a poem and make his or her own way through its form and content. [Simple, some of my poems may be, but never simplistic.]

A final collection - *Diary of a Time Traveller* - will coincide with the year of my 70th birthday in 2015. I am working on it already; should my prostate cancer catch up with me before then, my executor has instructions to go ahead and publish it under the Assembly Books imprint. - RNT © 2012

BIOGRAPHY:

Roger N. Taber was born in Gillingham (Kent) on December
21st 1945. In 1973, he graduated with an Honours degree in
English and American Literature at the University of Kent in
Canterbury [UK]. A librarian by profession, he has lived in
London [Kentish Town] since 1985 and is now retired.

Contact: rogertab@aol.com

INTERNET LINKS:

BLOGS:

http://rogertab.blogspot.com/
http://aspectsofagaymanslifeinverse.blogspot.com/
http://rogertaberfiction.blogspot.com

ONE & OTHER:

http://www.webarchive.org.uk/wayback/archive/2010022312
1732/oneandother.co.uk/participants/Roger_T

[Reading from the 4th plinth in Trafalgar Square, July 14th 2009]

YOU TUBE CHANNEL

http://www.youtube.com/rogerNtaber

DEDICATION

TO OSCAR WILDE
(1854-1900)

DE PROFUNDIS

I lay floating in an ocean of misery,
willing myself to drown
while dolphins kept me company
and Apollo lingered on

Sharks, they kept a hungry distance,
an albatross winged by,
while waves lent a gentle cadence
to twilight's lullaby

Went into freefall to the ocean floor
and would have stayed,
but Apollo demanded of me more
while the dolphins cried

I let them have their way if reluctantly,
screaming for their motivation,
peering into a misty-eyed mortality,
without rhyme or reason

No one answered my question though
I strained to hear,
then twilight let a cloud pass through
and I found a poem there

Body of straw in that ocean of misery,
willing myself to drown,
I read an ode to life, love and a history
of peace after wars hard won

It told how little in life ever comes easy
including death…
such is the fickle nature of humanity
and ways of godmother Earth

I felt a poet's passion take hold of me,
heard its voice in a seagull's cry,
swimming me across an ocean of misery
to walk kinder shores, head high

I woke in tears still drenching my pillow,
began (slowly) to recover;
at chinks in the blinds, winks from Apollo
assuring me the worst was over

Note: May 2010 saw the resignation of David Laws from the coalition government; it was very sad for him personally and for the country. It appears he broke the rules regarding MPs expenses in order to protect his privacy. Apparently, he had claimed rent for an apartment owned by a man with whom he had been in a relationship since 2001. He did not declare the relationship.

In this day and age, I cannot help wondering why so many public figures do their utmost to keep their sexuality private. Could it be they (especially men) feel there is (still) a stigma attached to their sexuality? Oh, but surely not in a society that insists it is fair as well as liberal minded? While political correctness demands such a possibility be hotly denied, I can well understand (if not agree) why anyone in the public eye should prefer to keep details of their private life...well, private. The media are always looking to have a field day with as much as a hint of scandal. Even so, celebrities and other public figures can do a lot to promote Gay Awareness in a world where gay men and women are still persecuted in various countries. Some do, of course, and all credit and thanks to them for it.

I wrote this poem long before the David Laws affair while in the latter stages of a fragile recovery from a severe nervous breakdown some 30+ years ago; my only revision has been to give it a title; for this, I have to thank my close friend Graham Collett who has also designed some book covers for me.

Most readers will, of course, be aware that the poem takes its title from an epistle written by Oscar Wilde, in a state of dark despair, to Lord Alfred Douglas during the latter days of his incarceration in Reading gaol. My poem, too, was written in a state of dark despair; writing it made a significant contribution to both my physical and spiritual survival.

Tragically, for Wilde, the worst was far from over.

RNT©2012

CONTENTS

PART ONE

LINES OF BEAUTY

LINES OF BEAUTY

Lines of beauty, emerging sunset;
sometimes red, pink or yellow;
my eyes feast on them and I taste
peace and love on my tongue;
stronger even than with first light,
I bond with the sun's last rays;
clouds may crowd its glory but not
the immortality of its poetry

No sunset is ever quite the same
nor any poem on a like theme;
the sky, like the earth, taking pride
in its subtle variations;
better, surely, to share differences
than compete with them?
More of us would to well to mull
over lines of beauty in a sunset

MASTERPIECE

Streaks of gold on a sheet
of charcoal grey;
patches of green glistening
like wet paint

Bear-like figures emerging
from hibernation;
birds calling our landscape
into question

Children unafraid of giants
resembling trees;
reflections in an artist's eye
on post-storminess

A joy, seeing Earth Mother
at work and play;
a privilege, feeling her brush
stroking us in

Masterpiece, left unfinished
to challenge critics
on imagination, watch them
arguing the signature

A POEM FOR ALL SEASONS
(For Klaus J. Gerken)[i]

Love is a poem that turns on eternity,
touching on a thousand themes,
perceiving a rare beauty in integrity

Forget prose testing us to extremity,
tearing us apart at the seams,
love is a poem that turns on eternity

Where some may see cruel ambiguity,
love lends us promising dreams,
perceiving a rare beauty in integrity

Where harsh words, rooted in bigotry,
and humanity not all it seems,
love is a poem that turns on eternity

When we fall, let's preserve our dignity
where Earth Mother s eye gleams,
perceiving a rare beauty in integrity

Where colour, creed, sex and sexuality,
life's darker comedy redeems,
love is a poem that turns on eternity,
perceiving a rare beauty in integrity

THE ENCHANTED WOOD

Kind ghosts, smiling at me
wherever I go…
among leaves of memory

'Keep it safe, the old tree'
they whisper low,
kind ghosts smiling at me

Close friends and family,
all springtime on show
among leaves of memory

On a nature trail to eternity,
where love's seeds grow,
kind ghosts smiling at me

If the self its own enemy,
let its colours show
among leaves of memory

Keeping such company,
the poet I would be;
kind ghosts smiling at me
among leaves of memory

WHERE THE PASSWORD IS PEACE

I am the rose dripping pearls
on a camomile lawn stretching
across fields and woodlands
where trees tell tales wiser men
and women than you or I
have passed on since Creation
to the world's poets, painters
and its music makers to re-create
in a spirit of celebration

I am the lame dove haunting
frantic urban streets reaching out
for a peace of mind as told
by the world's poets, painters
and its music makers...
to still the restless heart, restore
a flagging faith in humanity
much like the rose dripping pearls
on a camomile lawn

I am not whom you took me for
when first you tried to read my face,
unused as you are to seeing clear,
mistaking an iconic tablet of stone
for a camomile lawn stretching
beyond parameters of time and space
where the password is peace,
trees are heard telling tales and roses
seen dripping pearls

Look behind and within all you see
and find me, who am called Beauty

REFLECTIONS IN A GLASS EYE

There is a beauty in ugliness
only they can see
who can warm their hands at hell's hearth
and still feel an affinity
with God

In the ugliest of creatures
there beats a heart
and will to live more splendid than anything
thought up by the art
of egocentricity

In the foul-smelling swamp
of human desire
left to its own devices for want of any insight,
find a lotus flower
shaming us

Yes, an ugly side to beauty,
often seen as worldly,
invariably posing for the press at hell's hearth
and claiming an affinity
with God

There is a beauty, too, in beauty
that's a rare poetry,
braving the daily cat-walk of green-eyed gods,
yet can still feel empathy
with beggars

ALTERNATIVES

I looked for God in heaven
but did not find Him there,
looked again, in sun and rain
for Earth Mother

Some say it's, oh, so pagan,
as bad as being gay;
I just see myself as someone
looking nature's way

God is many things to many,
interpreting His conditions
for the good of all humanity
according to its religions

The sun rises, sets, rises again,
and no one take issue
nor that moon and stars shine
or songbirds sleep as we do

Let nature sue for harmony,
hear our confessions,
and we feed less on acrimony
spread by world religions

To wake, sleep and wake again
may or may not imply rebirth
and, yes, each to his or her own
but we share a common earth

Who looks for God in heaven
and does not find Him there
has but to look in sun and rain
for Earth Mother

See, too, nature assert its power
where humankind gone too far

TRAILING ROSES

Dawn, a golden haze
among trailing trellis roses;
trees, dripping rainbows
on grasshoppers signing in
another day

Rooftops, sheets of glass
where birds pause to preen
a feather or two before
taking off to help usher in
another day

Bubble wrap skies, cue
for sleepyheads to wonder
why on earth heaven
is raising the alarm for just
another day

Sun rising, world trailing
after trellis roses like a lover
left for dead…
yet to rediscover fool's gold
another day

By noon, trellis roses
getting up the noses of those
who know no better
than to repeat their mistakes
another day

At dusk, nature playing
its daily nocturne to anyone
who cares to listen,
dares even show a sad world
another way

THE RIBBON

As twilight favoured us
a misty golden rain,
a joyful hymn to peace
rose above its pain,
freely acknowledging
that we had come
to that last, lonely parting
at time's guileless whim,
bringing us, less prepared
than we should be
though each of us warned
enough of an eternity
stretching like a pink ribbon
in Earth Mother's hair
against a near-far horizon,
beckoning us where
the rich and poor, beggars,
(even thieves) along
with saints and murderers
come for a reckoning
they've spent temporality
earning or avoiding
on that axis of morality
known for bending
rules and taking advantage
of cloth and kin
over anxious to salvage
the spoils of Creation;
fading fast, that twilight,
waiting (not unlike us)
on moon or stars to light
up the darkness
so we can see a way clear

to be sure the ribbon
for Earth Mother's hair
is never forgotten...

Or love (ever) forsaken

AT THE END OF THE DAY

Sleepy sun like a yellow tee shirt
after a summer shower,
logo proclaiming peace and love;
songbirds on cue, soul of summer
bursting with pride and joy,
wishing us kind dreams and sleep

A pink glow infiltrating grey clouds,
tips of angels' wings
spying out the lie of borrowed time;
jet lag moon among laid back stars
telling tales on our humanity
to fill a wide-awake media's pockets

A grey squirrel turning over garbage
is quick to turn up its nose
at an envelope marked 'Top Secret';
kids trespassing on a new building site
unearth skulls, go-betweens
for this developer, that archaeologist

Night falls, harbinger of sleep waiting
in the wings, time's hopeful
understudy groomed for second best;
world's top rated spotted flogging
dead horses with Apollo's customised
tee shirt, come Armageddon

THE APPRENTICE

I am as clay
that can be shaped however
the potter chooses
and have little say in the matter
but must follow
where caring, firm hands lead
(in my best interests?)
while subtler firing needs
left unfulfilled

I am as steel,
shaped only with some difficulty
for another's ends,
yet the welder who knows how
to bend me to his will
does not hesitate to demonstrate
his skill if only to satisfy
an audience of but one person
in his sights

I am as poetry
that can be shaped however
the reader chooses,
led by the hand through a maze
of thoughts and feelings,
caring hands suggesting this way
or that, leaving us to make
our own fate nor judged for how
we turn out

Call me Individuality, best left to be
a star apprentice to Creativity

LINE OF VISION

If strands of grey in the hair turning white
and less subtle laughter lines in the face,
you smile, and my world is filled with light,
as tired limbs summon dignity and grace

If the voice sounding weaker than before,
its familiar lilt still sweet on the ear,
so this heart can but listen out for more,
for knowing that today (at least) we're here

Time, we know, always parts lovers too soon,
yet nurture with nature will have its way,
and who seeks among craters of the moon
will find flowers we planted there today

In good times and bad, see love's light endure,
nor shall even death's tears our vision blur

IN PRAISE OF SEA THRIFT

Guardians of our history,
looking out for us
among rocks by the sea

Shadows once the enemy,
now protectors,
guardians of our history

As natural as we to nudity,
rising, falling waves...
among rocks by the sea

Lovers, like fishes set free
from glass cages,
guardians of our history

Witness Apollo frantically
planting kisses...
among rocks by the sea

Careworn, fickle humanity
proofing its pages;
guardians of our history
among rocks by the sea

SEASIDE, THROUGH A RAIN CLOUD'S EYE

I see breakers crashing on the shore,
seagulls circling above,
face at windows of a nearby hotel
and a woman walking her dog

I see an ice-cream van doing no trade,
heads busy dodging umbrellas,
faces at windows of a nearby hotel
and a beggar being moved on

I see a windsurfer gathering speed,
seagulls keeping an eye,
faces at windows of a nearby hotel
and lovers pausing for a kiss

I see plastic shopping bags burst open,
their owner getting in a state,
faces at the window of a nearby hotel
and a man exit a Bookies, crying

I see cinemagoers pouring into a street,
frantically reaching for phones,
faces at windows of a nearby hotel
and the lovers having a quarrel

I see the woman's dog (not on a leash)
go chasing after a cat,
faces at the window of a nearby hotel
and the windsurfer taking a tumble

I see a watery sunlight breaking through
layers of cloud, shades of grey,
faces at windows of a nearby hotel
showing signs of coming alive

[Brighton, East Sussex, March 2010]

THE TIME KEEPER

Keeper of my time since the day
I first saw you, a beauty to the eye
more splendid than royalty, riding
on a white unicorn in pastures green
mountains or gently rolling hills,
Child of Avalon, Queen of Hearts,
carried on wings and a prayer
like wildly flowing hair in chariots
of fire

Keeper of my time since the day
I first heard you sing songs making
heaven ring out with such hopes
of spring, joys only summer days
can bring, dreams that autumn
cannot fulfil or winter kill, whatever
any God may have in mind for us,
left free to choose, for good or ill,
always

Keeper of my time since the day
I first followed you in a storm,
shared the violence of a passion
equal to death's own, nor less
a rage to live than ever stirs in me,
envious of rider-unicorn a place
in eternity, riding, rearing or simply
left to graze, my fickle mistress,
Lady of the Hours

Keeper of our tides in history,
the sea, the sea

A SEASONAL MAGIC

Often, as spring is fading,
I spot a face in clouds I know well,
as sure as a late lark working
the magic of its ages-old spell

Often, as summer is fading,
I hear a voice in my ears I know well,
as sure as a fine rain seducing
the trees with its ages-old spell

Often, as autumn is fading,
I feel caresses on my skin I know well,
as sure as a fair wind rising
to Earth Mother's ages-old spell

Often, as winter is falling,
I surrender to an embrace I know well,
as sure as home fires reworking
what passes for an ages-old spell

Where a season's colours fading
like the dream we knew only too well,
other lovers are discovering
the magic of its ages-old spell

THE CROWDED SKY

I've seen ghost riders
chasing sandmen into storm clouds
and leaves fly

I've seen ghost riders
throw a sandman into a dark place
and trees cry

I've seen ghost riders
pluck such as I from fragile shelters
and no one notice

I've seen ghost riders,
others like me into this sorry world's
worst nightmares

I've let ghost riders
drag me from my armchair, re-awaken
my consciousness

I've let ghost riders
rescue me from assault by prime time
TV advertising

I've let ghost riders
force me to face my more fragile selves
head-on

I've let ghost riders
trample a rainbow, watched it crumble,
only to re-assemble

One by one, ghost riders
falling away, till nothing left to say they
are even history...

Except me

MY HERO IS A TREE
(For Val Berry)[ii]

Leaves on my hero are budding,
the music of spring as sweet as ever heard;
swallows returning bring life
to field and valley, filling the lonely heart
with thoughts of love;
Leaves on my hero are singing
songs of summer as feisty as passion;
young folks laughing bring life
to field and valley, filling hearts growing old
with memories of love;
Leaves on my hero are turning
red and gold in the company of dreams,
swallows leaving, sure to return
to field and valley while hearts young and old
fly the colours of love;
Leaves on my hero are drifting
across time and space, world without end;
tears of pain, joy and hope
flying field and valley like bright eyed children
running with kites;
Leaves on my hero are budding.
the music of spring as sweet as ever heard;
swallows returning bring life
to field and valley, and new takes on old stories
we tell on love;
Leaves on my hero are singing
songs of summer as feisty as passion;
young folks laughing bring life
to field and valley, teasing hearts growing old
they know nothing of love;
Leaves on my hero are turning
red and gold in the company of dreams;

swallows leaving, sure to return
to field and valley while hearts young and old
fly the colours of love;
Leaves on my hero are drifting
across time and space, world without end;
tears of pain, joy and hope
flying field and valley, the children we were,
running with kites

BACK IN BUSINESS

Sometimes when I'm feeling low,
I'll enter paintings on walls,
engage with crowds at market fairs,
let history course my veins,
giving selfhood a new dimension
and fresh direction, letting
a lazy inner eye know, yes, we're
back in business

Or I might stroll along rugged cliffs,
communing with waves below,
pause to chat with a friendly peasant
whose lot more harsh
than I will ever know, text books
do justice or any sympathy
with poverty even begin to home
in on the real thing

An old farm house might invite me
to join its ghosts in a hearty meal,
the inimitable smell of home baking
lingering long after we're eaten,
reviving my other senses, replacing
lethargy with motivation
enough to find satisfaction in putting
imagination to work

PART TWO

LASTING IMPRESSIONS

LASTING IMPRESSIONS
(For Nuala & Christopher)[iii]

Once I heard a story
about a dream that never dies,
of all we hope to see
beyond love's tears and lies

Once I read poetry
about a love that never ends,
its spirit set free
from all the body but lends

Once I heard a song
that let fly my heart like a bird
soaring proud and strong
on the wings of every word

Once I saw a painting
of lovers in some long-ago time,
yet as real as if still living
the dream now yours and mine

Once I saw actors bring
love's ageless story to the stage;
a poem about our writing
its every word, turning every page

Come cut and thrust of all creation,
it's to love we look for inspiration

CLASSIC SOMERSET

Doone valley, classic fiction
for holiday images
conjuring true inspiration

Come any with a predilection
for turning nature's pages;
Doone valley, classic fiction

At Badgworthy Water, listen
out for Carver's rages
conjuring true inspiration

At Earth Mother's invitation,
share a Love of Ages;
Doone valley, classic fiction

Celebration of Lorna and John
(birds singing their praises)
conjuring true inspiration

Cream teas teasing imagination
to revisit R. D's pages;
Doone valley, classic fiction
conjuring true inspiration

[Note: Inspired by a visit to the setting of R. D. Blackmore's classic
novel , *Lorna Doone*.]

A POET'S SHREWSBURY

Follow the market trader's cry
across old Shrewsbury town
where the fickle Severn flows by

Discern in history's cloudy eye
scenes of Parliament v Crown;
follow the market trader's cry

At Laura's tower, dare lift high
the hem of Nature's gown
where the fickle Severn flows by

Swans over the English Bridge fly
with dive-bombing precision,
follow the market trader's cry

See sunset's flames lick at the sky
as if the grand abbey burning down
where the fickle Severn flows by

Ponder a war poet casting the die,
Darwin giving heaven cause to frown;
follow the market trader's cry
where the fickle Severn flows by

[Shrewsbury, August 2007]

[Note: I wrote this poem while in the lovely old town Shrewsbury to give a poetry reading.]

A MEASURE OF CREATIVITY

Like a folly satirising our history,
love takes to task its fears;
nature's last laugh on humanity

Find the world's blackest comedy
imposed on we poor actors
like a folly satirising our history

Glistening like a vision of eternity,
a lake of glad-sad tears;
nature's last laugh on humanity

Watch how feisty skies effectively
feed on the world's prayers
like a folly satirising our history

Hear the trees compose a melody
falling mostly on cloth ears;
nature's last laugh on humanity

Deception, left to cascade prettily
down centuries of applause,
like a folly satirising our history;
nature's last laugh on humanity

[Virginia Water, UK. May 9th 2009]

[Note: The folly at Virginia Water - albeit not the usual kind of
folly - provided inspiration for the cover design of my collection,
On the Battlefields of Love]

THE ZEN OF DISCERNMENT
(For Jim Howard)[iv]

Like ghosts, our years pass us,
(the mixed blessings of memory)
as hauntingly beautiful as stars

No lesser regard for science
than Earth Mother's finer poetry,
like ghosts, our years pass us,

Images of laughter and tears
finest art can only ever but copy,
as hauntingly beautiful as stars

No hopes wing more precious
than family and friends in harmony;
like ghosts our years pass us

Come birdsong to fine old trees,
so joy and pain creating our history,
as hauntingly beautiful as stars

As centuries turn nature's leaves,
so each human heart creates eternity
like ghosts, our years pass us,
as hauntingly beautiful as stars

WINGS OF A DOVE
(For Colleen Howard)[v]

The years, oh, how they fly by,
made to run the gamut of sun and rain
like doves in a blue-grey sky

All they teach, we well may try,
(mistakes, haunting us again and again);
the years, oh, how they fly by

Eager to earn love's sweeter cry,
we'll journey, too, among joy and pain
like doves in a blue-grey sky

Life, it will have us laugh and cry,
where love wipes our tears, moves us on;
the years, oh, how they fly by

Bonded to family and friends, a tie
lending us metaphor, rhyme and reason,
like doves in a blue-grey sky

Children of Earth, we live and die,
bring meaning to its bitter-sweet season;
the years, oh, how they fly by
like doves in a blue-grey sky

KEEPER OF THE FLAME

I pile on wood,
and the flames leap higher,
bringing us together
as we were that summer
we'd meet up again
and again to go swimming
in the sunshine,
walking in the rain,
playing with fire
from each dawn to sunset,
now flaring, now fading
like love's wistful voices,
its weepy echoes

I pile on wood,
and the flames are dancing,
lovers romancing
as we were that summer
we'd cherish
precious moments together,
each one stolen
from those who thought
they knew us,
yet never once suspecting
we were lovers,
not just best of friends
hamming it up

I run out of wood,
and too soon the flames start
to fall away
like an audience once a play
has reached an ending
well deserving of applause
even if no one cares
to admit the staged goings-on
were too close
for comfort, disturbing
vulnerable ghosts
ever tearful for being shut
in some secret closet

Fire smouldering, but a flicker
braving it out

THE GREEN MAN

Walking in woods one day,
a beautiful stranger came my way,
a youth dressed all in green,
sweet breath chasing clouds away,
in sunny hair, a leafy crown

The young man beckoned me
to take a path I'd not followed before;
I did just that, unhesitatingly,
so commanding, if fair, a look and air
of age-old majesty

Trees, brambles, wild flowers,
making an impressive if chaotic show,
we sprinted autumn's hours,
keeping pace with its bold amber glow,
undeterred by leafy showers

We came at last to a pretty glade
where the young man bade me lie down
on a spacious grassy bed
then lay beside me, took me for his own
and I, oh, so gladly responded

Pleasurably spent, I slept till dawn,
woke, not in the wood of our lovemaking,
(the Green Man, too, was gone)
but where once I'd be tossing and turning
for fear I was a bad person

A dream, yes, but also nature's way
of reassuring a youth so tormented by shame
there is none in being gay;
we have but to give the Green Man a name
and live to love another day

THE DANCER UPSTAIRS

I lay in bed,
listening to the music upstairs,
no wish to sleep,
my thoughts dancing in tune
with pretty dance steps;
now gliding across my world
like an ice queen;
now gate-crashing my privacy
like a rock star

I lay in bed
in a frenzy, like the music upstairs,
growing more frantic
every second that images of you
take the floor;
now introducing me to your world's
choreography;
now swinging us into an ecstasy
of rock 'n' roll

I lay in bed,
relating to gentler sounds above,
as if the music, like me
has finally grown weary of passion
and seeks peace;
now lifting me on wings of grace
like a dove to nest;
now asking with sweet echoes
that I cave in to love

Hearts beating in time with nature's refrain,
I turned to kiss you as we listened to the rain

ELLA SINGS THE BLUES

How will it be when I'm dead?
Will I hear music playing in my head,
see a dove fly by in a clear blue sky,
hear a newborn baby's very first cry
and Ella singing?

How will it be when I die?
Will I wing with the dove, oh, so high
that I can look down and see
those I've loved crying rivers for me
or rivers run dry?

How will it be when I'm gone?
World keeps turning and life goes on
so where does that leave me,
courtesy (hopefully) of a spirituality
come clean?

How will it be when I'm dead?
will I still compose poems in my head,
grieve a sorry world lost its way
for listening to what its 'betters' say
who haven't a clue?

I'll never know until I'm dying,
but when I am be sure I'll be flying high
among doves with you, listening
out for every newborn baby's crying
and Ella singing

THE GUARDIAN

Where snow is falling snow on snow
and the world is a lonely place,
a woman in white would softly go,
and were we to see her face,
we would know she comes for us

Where acid rain defies flowers to grow
and the world is a lonely place,
a woman in tears would softly go,
and were we to see her face,
we would know she comes for us

Where summer breezes gently blow
and the world is a lonely place,
a woman in green would softly go,
and were we to see her face,
we would know she comes for us

Where autumn makes a splendid show
and the world is a lonely place,
a woman in gold would softly go,
and were we to see her face,
we would know she comes for us

Loved ones gone and we need to know
why the world is a lonely place;
it's a woman called Hope tells us so,
and were we to see her face,
we would know she comes for us

Look where she comes and see her face,
let this world be a less lonely place

IN CHERRY BLOSSOM TIME

Cherry blossom and empty crisp packets
drifting by on a breeze

Empty crisp packets, like lonely people
drifting by on a street

Streets, like lines on the faces of martyrs
drifting by on clouds

Clouds, trying hard not to cry for a world
getting by on crutches

Crutches, supporting old guard politicians
getting by on half lies

Half lies, camouflage for good intentions
getting by for centuries

Centuries, a colourful history of cleaning
other people's windows

Windows on religions swearing to their fruit
like cherry blossom

Cherry blossom and empty crisp packets
drifting by on a breeze

MOON UNDER THE WATER

She strolled as silent as light
to stand by my side;
together we watched moonlight
surf a rolling tide

She took my hand, held it tight,
said not a word
as we watched a jaded starlight
across the water glide

She led me to the water's edge,
shadows dipping low,
night train sobbing on a bridge
like a war widow

She squeezed my hand, let it go,
trod softly on moonlight,
its sylph-like waves grieving so
for the death of night

She did not call on me to follow,
yet I heard her voice
filing a heart left dark and hollow
for given no choice

She sung a song of truth and lies,
urging I live life to the full
where moonlight's bridge of sighs
gives way to dawn's chorale

I returned home, day's light clear
if cheeks stained with tears,
mail train raising a hearty cheer
for the world's survivors

READ THE HAND, WRITE US UP

There's a hand that caresses the first buds of spring
and bids them grow

It moves among summer corn in time for harvesting
by courtesy of Apollo

Where autumn's leaves making ready for its turning,
it bestows a blessing;

When winter brings us to our knees, of life despairing,
it beckons us to spring

Where we run the gamut of love, hate, peace and war,
find, too, Earth Mother

But let a fair hand caress and smooth its troubled brow
or we destroy each other

The question arises, dare we bite the hand that feeds us,
face the consequences?

Or do we accept it in a spirit of goodwill to all humanity,
put aside our differences?

Beware, or the hand that rocks the cradle may let it drop,
our world breaking up

It's to read the hand that's writing us up we need to learn
or else…Armageddon

THE SADDEST SWINGER IN TOWN

I am a friend to none,
but embrace all, yet it is not
out of vindictiveness
I swing for every man, woman
and child on the streets
of a world fast losing the plot
when it comes down
to getting its priorities right
(looking after its own)

Some call me The Teaser,
calling on Life to flirt with Mercy,
dragging kindly souls
deserving far better than this
to an untimely death;
small comfort in Earth Mother's
lasting kiss for those
left to grieve for the greater
of love's tragedies

I spare none, but feast
on shadows, waters of the womb
and leftover dreams;
Yet, even I can be beaten,
forced to retreat,
were the world to take arms
against its penchant
for glossy storylines, take issue
with home truths

Poverty, the saddest swinger in town,
(can't be helped, best left alone?)

THE MARRYING KIND?

Some marriages are made in heaven
others in hell,
or (needs must) political transfusion

Find love, free to rise to the occasion
and doing well;
some marriages are made in heaven

Witness compromise beat disillusion
on a media swell
or (needs must) political transfusion

Credit democracy with real ambition
and looks to kill;
some marriages are made in heaven

A brave new world defying confusion,
if policies yet to sell,
or (needs must) political transfusion

Time enough to see cynics on the run
among history's free-for-all;
some marriages are made in heaven
or (needs must) political transfusion

Note: On May 13th 2010 the Liberal Democrats and Conservatives
announced their agreement for a Coalition Government in the UK.

SPRING CHORUS

Cheers for a royal wedding,
like flowers of the earth;
joys of love's eternal spring

World, its lovers applauding
since birth and rebirth;
cheers for a royal wedding

Where young lovers pledging
a sacred troth,
joys of love's eternal spring

Nation, to its Family bringing
comforts of its hearth;
cheers for a royal wedding

If royalty, its hardships wring,
make time, too, for mirth,
joys of love's eternal spring

Find in every tear, a blessing
as a gentle rain to earth;
cheers for a royal wedding;
joys of love's eternal spring

Note: Written to celebrate the wedding of HRH Prince William and
Ms Catherine Middleton, April 29th 2011.]

AMONG SHADES OF EVERGREEN

Among shades of evergreen
at nature's heart,
find jewels fit for a queen

All freedom, since time began,
on red alert
among shades of evergreen

Come dew on a peace rose seen
at each new day's start,
find jewels fit for a queen

See lives, loves and tears fallen
to death's random dart
among shades of evergreen

Come a spirituality wiping clean
history's darker part,
find jewels fit for a queen

Cherish first hints of spring, icon
for humanity's re-start;
among shades of evergreen,
find jewels fit for a queen

[Note: This villanelle was written in 2011 to celebrate the respective 85th and 90th birthdays of Her Majesty The Queen and HRH Prince Philip that year.]

FIRST AMONG DIAMONDS

Let diamonds be forever
(up for grabs as time goes by)
it's love binds us together

Some ties none can sever,
come family, friends, country;
let diamonds be forever

If we ask of each other
all duty commands us, you and I,
it's love binds us together

Our privilege, an endeavour
to shine as stars in a summer sky;
let diamonds be forever

Let us never say 'never'
(run the gamut, we can only try);
it's love binds us together

May we see our way clear,
embrace an enduring spirituality;
let diamonds be forever,
it's love binds us together

[Note: Written in celebration of Her Majesty The Queen's Diamond
Jubilee, 2012.]

THE SHINING

Boy drops a shiny new coin
into gutter and watches it dive
down a drain;
Boy chases after The Shining,
is soon swimming
for thrills with sewer rats
smelling of roses

Boy reaches an expanse
of sea, a glittering star-like icon
on waves sure to tease,
making sure it always stays
just out of reach
no matter how well he swims
or how far

Boy whose coin it was
dropped down a drain and swam
an odyssey smelling
of roses - grew up and learned
the hard way
how swimming with sewer rats
ain't no fun

No surprises then
that Boy became a banker, having
already learned
how to swim with sewer rats
after The Shining
and succeed in coming up
smelling of roses

DECONSTRUCTING CYBERIA

Who (now) has the faintest idea
what's right, wrong, true, false, hearsay,
about goings-on in the media?

Is no one safe from the blagger,
and whose phone was hacked into today?
Who (now) has the faintest idea?

Seedy types are exploiting Cyberia,
its millions of everyday tourists led astray
about goings-on in the media

Can intrusion into any private arena
be justified by pushing it Joe Public's way?
Who (now) has the faintest idea?

If one malpractice leads to another,
what's the right take on what is or isn't okay
about goings-on in the media?

Though no person or enterprise bigger
than a Free Press left to have an honest say,
who (now) has the faintest idea
about goings-on in the media?

[London: July 2011]

[Note: Written during the early days of news breaking about the
phone hacking scandal in relation to News International.]

LIVE METAPHOR, DEAD ENDS

At a wall dripping blood and tears,
humanity, for its sins, dares not forget;
live metaphor for the world's fears

Where democracy disappears,
political ambition refuting Terror's debt
at a wall dripping blood and tears

Where humanity to victory steers,
political agendas conspiring to thwart;
live metaphor for the world's fears

Divisions perpetuated for years,
brave new worlds apart since last we met
at a wall dripping blood and tears

Where Time's kinder mist clears,
see guards with orders to shoot on sight;
live metaphor for the world's fears

Where Freedom's fair head rears,
its worst enemy some socio-cultural tenet
at a wall dripping blood and tears;
live metaphor for the world's fears

[Note: On August 13th 2011, hundreds gathered at a central
memorial in Berlin to mark the 50th anniversary of the building of
the Berlin Wall and remember all those who died .]

WATERSHIP DOWN REVISITED

I ran like a frightened rabbit,
a once-friendly darkness all but
choking my lungs;
every exit blocked, no escape,
sentenced to death in the pages
of a novel

Panic-stricken now, desperate
to feast my eyes on one glimpse
of freedom;
finally, surrendering to despair,
I paused, all but ready to see how
my story ends

Suddenly, the faintest memory
of some long-ago spring charged
my ailing heart;
calling upon a half buried will,
I somehow managed to chase it
down the last tunnel

In fresh air and warm sunshine
I found the peace that closes eyes
and lets dreams pass
where, oh, but we would follow,
give reality the slip and be a hero
in someone else's novel

[Note: Inspired by the classic animal fantasy novel by Richard
Adams.]

BETWEEN LAND AND SEA
(For Al-Antony Moody)[vi]

At the sea's edge, I met a boy like me
who smiled, said let's be friends;
we laughed, dipped toes in the water
and splashed each other;
later on, we taught ourselves to swim
blue skies smiling down at us
as we laughed, chased fish in the water
and splashed each other

At the sea's edge, I met a youth like me
who smiled, said let's be friends;
we laughed, dipped toes in the water
and splashed each other;
later on, we stripped naked in a cove,
blue skies smiling down at us
as we laughed, chased crabs in the sand
and tumbled each other

At the sea's edge, I met a man like me
fishing for the moon in the water;
a dark wave came, the mirror smashed,
pieces everywhere;
later on, a near deafening cannonade
sent us scuttling for shelter…
and (finally) a man who looks like me
found it in Earth Mother

PART THREE

OPENING UP TO LOVE

OPENING UP TO LOVE

The first thing I saw as I opened my eyes,
the love in my mother's face;
I hadn't yet learned the words to describe,
but sensed I was in a safe place

The first thing I felt as I opened my eyes,
my mother's arm cradling me;
I hadn't yet learned the words to describe,
but sensed it was a good place to be

The first thought I had as I opened my eyes,
that journey's end is but the start
of living by and learning words to describe
the love in Earth Mother's heart

In a world without words, only its first cries
find reassurance in well-meant promises

CASTAWAYS

Washed up on an island
in a misty dream,
passing centuries shadowing us,
wings across golden sand

Game to explore an island
in a misty dream,
fair memories waving back at us,
castle flags on golden sand

Last seen kissing on an island,
sea mist closing in,
too soon, time's tide covering us,
footprints on golden sand

Closer to nature on an island,
(love's lasting dream)
earth's descant surely winging us,
seabirds across golden sand

As golden sand to ocean waves
are the world's lovers...
though humankind run the gamut
of nature's grudges against it

[Note: I am a shameless Doris Day fan and wrote this poem after
listening to her singing *Love's Little Island*.]

COCOON

Out of a golden twilight,
you stepped into my dreams,
took me in your arms

You hugged and kissed me,
gave my loneliness new heart
from the very start

In that gentle, golden mist,
you led me into a lovemaking
that was breathtaking

Later, you held me close,
wrapped yourself around me;
cocoon of spirituality

In the folds of a pink sunset,
we gay lovers left our dreams
to Earth Mother's charms

Come dawn's first light,
odds against us cruelly stacked,
cocoon (for now) intact

[Note: This poem was written in 1973, rediscovered in 2010 and
slightly revised.]

CUSTOM MADE

We dream of being together,
looking after each other,
seizing each day,
and it really doesn't matter
we're gay

We dream of living together,
looking after each other,
leading the way
for those to whom it matters
they're gay

We dream of staying together,
looking after each other,
come what may,
and it really doesn't matter
what folks say

Dreams, bringing us together,
looking after each other,
realised every day,
custom made for all lovers,
straight or gay

A GUIDING LIGHT

Love, a guiding light
through a mist of days
come darkest night

Though I take fright
of life's shadowy maze,
love, a guiding light

Once blind, I have sight,
alert to false trails always
come darkest night

Where doves take flight,
and douse a sunset's blaze,
love, a guiding light

Like wrong and right,
upon conscience it preys
come darkest night

Reason not the right;
where a heart will, it stays;
love, a guiding light
come darkest night

MAKING SURE OF LOVE

I built a sandcastle for you,
but you kicked it down with infant feet,
and made me cry buckets

I wrote a love poem for you,
but you threw a typical teenage tantrum,
and tore it into tiny pieces

I composed a pop song for you,
and everyone loved it except the person
for whom it was intended

I painted a portrait of you,
but you didn't care for the way I see you,
and cold-shouldered me

I made a solemn promise to you
that I'd love you forever, no matter what,
and we kissed

We made love together, bonding
with eternity, transcending a born intimacy,
and centuries-old creativity

Together, we built a castle
to withstand all temporal waves, reaffirm
the spirituality of creativity

GIFT-WRAP

It looked a long way;
some people said it was the wrong way;
though we cared what they said,
went ahead, did our own thing instead
and be damned...
joined your body to mine, let it patch up
a gaping hole in the soul
and you knew damn well I'd not been
saving myself for you at all

It didn't matter to us,
two of a kind, dancing mouth to mouth
on the same damn smile
willing us, daring us, the last damn mile
on a one way trip to heaven
some people said would see us burn in hell;
we didn't care at all
so long as we were wrapped up together,
making love forever

Time wasn't on our side
just stayed long enough to expose
the beauty and glory of a love
inspiring sex of a kind to blow the mind
into pieces spinning time and space,
across galaxies where same sex lovers
have no need for a defence
against people who haven't a clue
how it is for us

Forever sounds a long time;
some people said it was the wrong time
but we didn't listen,
did our own thing till you left me on my own
spinning time and space
across galaxies where same sex lovers
aren't even expected to explain
to people who haven't a clue how come
I'm still joined to you

Every dawn, noon, sunset and darkness
wraps me up, signs me with your kisses

HANDS ON

It's love sustains me every day;
bad times, good times, whatever,
though my lover passed away

It doesn't matter that I am gay,
there are ties death dare not sever;
it's love sustains me every day

I listen to what the season's say,
and take my cue from Earth Mother
though my lover passed away

Though some despair I'll not pray
to God, cynical of my trust in nature,
it's love sustains me every day

Where there's a will, there's a way,
as surely as spring shall follow winter;
it's love sustains me every day

Shaping my will to live, like clay
in the hands of a centuries-old potter,
it's love sustains me every day
though my lover passed away...

IN PIECES

After the song died, a part of me
died too as I contemplated the remains
in my glass of a love affair
that spread wings, played neighbour
to clouds among birds of the air
only to feel...a bullet through its body,
fired expertly by someone you say
you love more than you ever loved me,
loving you with a fiery passion
whose flames relentlessly devouring
every nuance of feeling in this ruin
of a lover left but contemplating ghosts
in a near empty glass of wine...
wondering where did I go so wrong
when all I wanted was to listen
to a love song with you, and I did
but it died, so I must drink up
and feel my way around a near empty
wine glass...till nothing left of us?

In despair, I threw and broke the glass,
watched rise from its pieces
a love song like a phoenix from ashes,
and drops of wine coursed
through my every vein till I, too,
came alive again

If a love song fades, its spirit never dies,
nor can it survive long in a wine glass

INSIDER OUTRAGE

See true lovers pursued by outrage
for defying a cultural bigotry,
find their blood on its every page

Let 'honour' rewrite each page,
confident in its hypocrisy;
see true lovers pursued by outrage

Lovers' sweet kisses dare assuage
the heart's hurts but briefly;
find their blood on its every page

See desire transcended by courage,
lent to all injustices by history;
see true lovers pursued by outrage

Where religion vents unholy rage
for all said to shame humanity,
find their blood on its every page

Let honour dare with love engage,
and celebrate family unity;
see true lovers pursued by outrage;
find their blood on its every page

[Written with a young couple in mind forced to flee their families
because they are on opposite sides of a cultural divide. One is an
Indian, the other a Pakistani; both were born in the UK.]

NO APPETITE FOR PEARS

I am the tear that lingers on the eye
as it peers through the mirror of its days
and cares not for all it sees,
blots out dark clouds and acid rain,
brings joy once again
to the heart once placed in the care
of others, happier times
to embrace and share, sure to last
and (like love) endure

I am the tear that lingers on the cheek
having expected to receive dawn's kisses,
but left smarting instead
from a slap by the cold light of day
in return for deeds played out
with best intentions but resulting
in such livid recriminations
as give rise to altercation that defies
either logic or justification

I am the smile that lingers on the lips
after apologies gladly accepted, if rather
late in the day, but better by far
than stubbornly corroding a mind,
anxious to recover all it has lost
yet never quite appreciated...until
fingers reaching for the phone
refuse to dial my number and life
goes pear shaped

Where dawns quickly pass and sunsets dip,
I'm there for you who am called Friendship

LOVE IN A MIST

Even the sun took time to cry
as we parted, you and I,
not knowing if we'd ever meet again,
barely seeing for a misty rain

We swore to write every day,
be true, come what may,
though a fear we wouldn't meet again
chilling us, like a misty rain

I watched you go, saw you turn,
felt blown kisses start to burn
a hole in my heart where you had been,
now gone in a misty rain

The sun stayed behind a cloud;
as I named my love aloud,
leaving a summer wind to bear my pain
on the wings of a misty rain

Autumn passed and winter too,
yet I heard no word from you,
despairingly let all but one hope wane
as I strolled in a misty rain

Suddenly, the sun reappeared
from behind a grieving cloud;
there we were, we dead flowers reborn
in the sweetest of spring rain

We heard birds sing out that day
for lovers, straight and gay,
echoes of Earth Mother's eternal refrain
though, at times, a misty rain

ON THE INTIMATE NATURE OF STAR GAZING

Once, I wished on a falling star
as lovers the world over will do,
that soon we can be together,
knowing you'll be wishing too

The star vanished in the night
though others kept me company
as I wondered how you are,
knowing you're thinking of me

I felt even closer to you then
than at times when you're near,
fighting back tears, the pain
of star-crossed lovers everywhere

No heaven frowns upon us
(even the Old Man takes our part)
but the world's prejudices
would force us, gay lovers, apart

For now, they may have won
a battle or two, but never say die,
for love will see us through
in this as in darker years gone by

For every person wishing us ill,
others echo Earth Mother who calls
to let live love and fulfil
its dreams for every star that falls

May we each find joy and peace
in one another, wherever we may be;
make the world a kinder place,
let all its star-crossed lovers go free

RIVER OF DREAMS, RHYTHM OF LIFE

I recall one long lovely summer
when we'd stroll beside a river,
discovering more about each other
than we ever knew before

I recall how we lay in long grass,
shared our first shy, gay kiss,
soaking us with more happiness
than we ever knew before

I recall how our naked bodies
mingled with butterflies,
a more glorious heat embracing us
than we ever knew before

In your arms, my cheek against
your bare chest…
in nature's hands more blessed
than we ever knew before

Before we dressed, another kiss
could but let the grass
play a sweeter song on our bodies
than we ever knew before

We walked, hand in hand, along
the river bank, its love song
ours to keep, righting any wrong
others had done us before

Years on, we stroll by a river,
chatting with each other,
your ghost and I, joined together
as we never were before

TAKING ON HALLOWEEN

One Halloween at a full moon,
come the witching hour,
live wires humming our tune

You had left me, oh, too soon,
life tasting, oh, so sour,
one Halloween at a full moon

Walking on in an autumnal rain
like a winter shower,
live wires humming our tune

A hand slipped gently into mine
like spring to a flower,
one Halloween at a full moon

Love, treading a rare time-line,
kept me company there,
live wires humming our tune

It lifted me, a spirit all but divine,
sure to last forever,
one Halloween at a full moon,
live wires humming our tune

LISTENING TO LOVE

Love gave me flowers
that faded away;
Love gave me kisses
that faded away;
Love told me any doubts
would fade away

Love did not mind
we're gay

People took your flowers
and threw them away;
People scorned our kisses,
called us names;
People warned us how we
would rue the day

Some people mind
we're gay

The language of flowers
speaks of love;
The heat of your kisses
speaks of love;
Love insists people to put
their doubts away

SPIRIT OF LOVE

At the moment of my death,
we'll make love again, just as
when our first twilight fell,
late summer leaves like a shower
of September rain, nature
casting a spell to keep us safer
than Holy Books dare tell

At the moment of my death,
we'll make love again, creating
as much joy and more
than it has given us, we chosen,
meant to fly time and space,
any separation but a homing-in
on some glorious horizon

At the moment of my death,
our love will surely kill all pain,
be as a tree in blossom,
its springtime come again, though
a storm play tricks on its light,
for I shall rise above any threat
to return where first we met

At the moment of my death,
the spirit of love will leave a mark
much like a smile on my pillow,
and I'll be guided by Earth Mother
to your side, she who kept faith
with us while we lived, as we two
stayed true to each other

Death may flirt with us night and day
yet will see us right, straight or gay

WAKING UP TO LOVE

There's a tree in a field
that sings me a love song
every time I'm sitting
where it rises from the ground;
listen and you'll hear
the lyric of a love song hanging
on a dream lost and found

By a tree in a field,
we wrote our first love song,
bodies entwining
as we lay there on the ground,
sharing with the birds
such joy, such passion, hanging
on a dream lost and found

There's a tree in a field
that watched us kiss and part,
not daring to believe
as we lay there on the ground
how gay love might
survive a world left but hanging
on dreams lost and found

To a tree in a field,
we returned to write a love song,
bodies entwining
as we lay there on the ground,
sharing with the birds
such joy, such passion, a waking
dream lost and found

PART FOUR

GAY IN THE GARDEN

GAY IN THE GARDEN

Fairest of flowers
found in spring's garden,
this love of ours

No ivory towers
but temples of passion,
fairest of flowers

Pride in colours
by nature freely given,
this love of ours

Like spring hours
from winter's grave risen;
fairest of flowers

Temporal powers
may rage but cannot ruin
this love of ours

Where bigotry cowers,
begs Earth Mother's pardon;
fairest of flowers,
this love of ours

[Note: I was born in Kent (Gillingham) often called 'The Garden of England'.]

AS IF...

They say he died of AIDS
and that's why some people speak of him
as if he were a dog that caught rabies
and had to be put down

He was a good man
some people say, often whispering in my ear
(as if loath to confide a great sin)
that he was gay

He was a kind man
some people seem anxious I should believe,
as if making reparation of the kind
worn on a sleeve

He was an honest man
some people waste no time in pointing out,
as if on the defensive after being
caught out in a lie

He was a friend, who died
of AIDS although some people will not say that,
as if in denial of a word that deserves
they get it right

A good, kind, honest friend
dies of AIDS and still people blaming gay men,
as if any minority ever had a monopoly
on promiscuity

AN ELEMENTARY TAKE ON EXPRESSIONISM

Gay, homosexual, queer;
these are words we are likely
to hear anywhere
because that's where you'll find us
(anywhere)
though I (personally) have to say
I prefer to have it said
of me I'm 'gay' because it's how
I see my sexual identity

'Homosexual' makes me feel
like a test tube specimen on some
research laboratory table,
exploration into an explanation
for cause, even cure
where genetics (and nature)
are only too happy
to explain away the vocabulary
of sexual identity

'Queer' conjures bleak memories;
dark closet days and society's misuse
of the word,
a closed-minded world of abuse
towards those of us
seeking (and finding) love
among our own sex
where small minds unfit for purpose
anxious to vilify us

Times change, our words passing
from meaning to meaning like bees
to flowers, children
to adulthood, attitudes maturing
(I'd like to say)
to peace and love enduring,
abuses of language
(people too) discovering the poetry
of sexual identity

Let the poetry natural to all of us
have its way, no matter what its critics
may have to say
about our use of rhyme, none at all
or socio-cultural expectancy...
Each poem and person to their time
and a spirit of creativity
that is no more a 'sin' or 'crime'
than sexual identity

ANTHOLOGY OF TEARS

Your mouth on mine, your spirit
invading my dreams, my conventional life
ripped apart at the seams,
I began to see what I hadn't felt able
to acknowledge for years,
that sadness is not the only cause for tears
but joy, too, debunking fears
instilled in me by ritual, threat and bribes
of salvation (my reward in 'Heaven')
demanding I recognize wrong from right,
never go where angels fear to tread,
always let Holy words have the last say
and avoid people who are gay

Your raw boldness entered me,
a roughness like sandpaper burning me up,
yet it was not for this my tears fell
but on feeling my body assume a new form,
its contours honed to something
beautiful, no mere glossy cover for anyone
to read but an art form likely to last
centuries in minds open to expressions
of individuality as well its privacies,
respectful of inspiration and aspiration,
no matter how some rate its chances
for salvation (whatever they mean by that)
or in terms of 'moral' judgement

You filled me with a rare passion,
who had been kept behind bars, supposedly
for my own protection, but you divined
a pain I could not share, broke into my prison
that did not even have a name

and showed me how not everyone's truth
is the same nor any shame
in going against this version or that so long
as we believe right is on our side;
better by far (surely?) than to have stayed put,
lied for appearances sake...
and what's wrong with taking a same sex lover,
making the most of who we are?

Yet, come the body's joy for our lovemaking,
let tears fall, too, for those (still) kept waiting

DIY

Once, ties that bind
lay broken, the last star snuffed out,
harsh words spoken in anger
stubbornly refusing to be put to rout
by an army of emotions
demanding I stay, put things right
where (without meaning to)
I'd said only what was right for me,
all but forgetting you

Once, ties that bind
lay as corpses under the same sheets
where we came together,
planning our future, listening out
for a dawn chorus
we never heard for words
spilling on our pillows
from lips we had kissed so tenderly
making you turn from me

Once, ties that bind
ran barefoot into a low, misty dawn
without care or thought
for their salvation, crushing them
among dead grasshoppers
in a frenzy of shamed retreat after
hearing you answer, 'No way!'
for letting the world in on the secret
that we two are gay

Ah, but ties that bind
once broken can yet be repaired
with the patience and skill

brought to lovers the world over
since time began
by those called in with a will to craft
their reconstruction
with tools of its ancient art passed
generation to generation

For every tie left broken by despair,
in each of us, a born ability to repair

AN AUTUMN KINDLING

Autumn is a sad time, some say,
yet it's a glad time of year for me,
recalling how one cold October
brought us a gloriously sunny day
when we paused, total strangers,
to watch squirrels in a tree at play

The tree, it was a pretty evergreen,
its shiny leaves smelling of summer,
recalling how one gorgeous June
I'd met a stunningly handsome man,
misread a one-night stand as love,
swore how I'd never go there again

The squirrels were a sight to see,
seemed unconcerned by our laughter;
we caught each other's lively eye
and your smile, it stirred ashes in me
till a long dead fire began to flicker,
the autumn wind blow far less coldly

We chatted for a while, took a photo
of the playful squirrels on our phones
till they scampered way out of sight;
nothing else for it now but part and go
our separate ways, yet we lingered,
and in your eyes, I saw my fire's glow

Winter days are cheerless, some say,
yet they're a glad time of year for me,
recalling how one golden October
blessed us with a glorious autumn day
when we paused, we total strangers,
to watch squirrels in a tall pine at play

The tree, oh, the prettiest evergreen,
its shiny leaves smelling of summer,
already re-working my life history,
telling the squirrels all about two men
getting really cosy and warm if shyly,
and plainly intending to go there again

FINDERS, KEEPERS

It was a bleak wintry day,
heart hanging low from snow clouds above
with nothing to say
but how there's really no counting on love;
I just couldn't get warm,
longed for your arms to hug and embrace me
but all I had was a dream
and yesterday's carrot-nose snowman
grinning inanely

Even a robin was grieving
as if, suddenly, February was too much to bear
and where, oh, where was spring?
No one here to ask, not even Earth Mother
as branches of an oak tree
groaned under the weight of fresh snow,
empathising with me
if but a crumb of comfort where my love
dare not go

The lake, it was frozen over,
ducks and moorhens waddling across pearly ice;
I ran then, for solace and shelter,
only to find myself outside your house;
'Knock on the door,' the robin sang
flying low overhead as if sounding out my youth,
its song no longer weak but strong,
as our love had been before challenged
by some deeper truth

I glanced back at the oak tree,
but it was the snowman, resolved to catch my eye,
and still grinning away at me,
that challenged me to give gay love a try.
I never did knock on the door;
suddenly, you were there for me, arms flung wide,
and I knew we'd be as once before
when the oak saw us find what no snow
could ever hide

FLESH AND BLOOD

When we told my parents
we are gay and in love,
the looks they flung us said it all,
their words fraught
with anger, pain and distress,
urging us to think again
about just what it would mean
to fly in the face of religion,
insult God and, oh, for what?

Desires of the flesh
overriding all human decency
(unnatural at that)

When we told your parents
we are gay and in love,
the looks they flung us said it all,
tumbling over words
conveying their happiness,
hopes that we will
know the same joys of love
that had been theirs
for years and, oh, for what?

Desires of the flesh
mindful of all human decency
playing its part

When my parents met yours
over dinner one night,
the looks they flung each other
did not augur well
for an entertaining evening,

but yours won mine over
with their no-nonsense talking
about living, loving,
sharing and, oh, but all that!

Desires of the flesh
with all that's good and decent
at its heart

[Note: I told only my mother I was gay during the years I mostly
stayed in the closet; same sex relationships had been illegal until
1967 in the UK where attitudes remained hardened towards gay
people, especially men. She warned me against telling anyone else.
Thankfully, the times they are a-changing; for some of us at least, in
some parts of the world.]

FOUND WANTING

When people ask why I'm gay,
I tell them I was born this way

People say it can't be true,
any God has better things to do
than create distorted images
to blot humankind's copybook,
rewrite history's pages,
make religions take a long look
at themselves, leave cultures
to those power-hungry vultures
that love to preach and lead,
assuming their authority as read

People suggest my sexuality
is irreconcilable with spirituality;
they, so blessedly taken in
by interpretations of Holy Books,
a case for eternity that brooks
no argument among those afraid
of condoning, let alone trying
to understand bigotry they're sold
by those we're told know better
how best to live with one another

People accuse me of blasphemy
(at best, a penchant for immorality)
and I have no clear defence
for what has to be a clear distortion
of what the Creator had in mind
for humankind, and I born as I am.
Ah, but agreeing involves seeing
there is a place for every one of us,

human creatures all, regardless
of colour, creed, sex or sexuality

Who will put humanity to the test,
and deny it found gravely wanting?

GAY MEN DON'T DO STUFFY

As we walked down
my street together, you held my hand;
people flung us dirty looks,
because they didn't understand
about falling in love

Outside my front door,
you gave me a big hug and kissed me;
passers-by made rude noises
because they didn't have a clue
about falling in love

As I fumbled for my key,
you shouted to the street how you felt
about me, and neighbours
turned up their noses at us because
it's what they do best

As I closed the door after us,
children playing hopscotch in the street
waved a cheery 'hello'
as if warning us to take no notice
of their stuffy parents

Once inside, we ran upstairs,
laughingly, carefree, still hand in hand,
shutting out a world
that didn't want to understand
gay men falling in love

[Note: Life is looking much better for many gay people while others
are still being persecuted for their sexuality world-wide.]

AN EDUCATION

I gave little thought
to sexuality until one day at school,
a classmate brushed against me
in the showers, causing a Tsunami
of mixed feelings to descend
on me, carry me away, refuting
every thought and lesson
I'd been taught in the best interests
of so-called 'Education'

I had to turn away
so he would not see or (worse) let on
to others how my sexuality
had responded to the heat and silk
of his splendid body
as, naked, we washed ourselves clean
though some would say
I was the victim of a temptation
to let my inner self 'sin'

I resisted temptation,
but no victim was I that day, only shown
an alternative way to live, love,
and fulfil what I had long suspected
was desire in me, but rejected
as an unknown quantity, preferring
to keep to safe, well worn paths
in the preferred manner and direction
of so-called 'Education'

I learned a much valued lesson that day,
acknowledged I am gay

KISS AND TELL

Your first kiss stripped my conscience bare
and reconstructed it, layer by finer layer

Your next kiss peeled away guilt of a Youth
that never quite came to terms with truth

More kisses instilled in me a peace of mind
my heart often warned I might never find

Other kisses showed me a brave new world
then took me there, its humanity revealed

Your mouth, it lit in me a bonfire of passion
reducing life's agony to a smouldering ruin

Your kisses flood me with beautiful dreams
where nightmares once tore at life's seams

Each kiss leaves my heart soaring like a dove;
where it sang the Blues, now it sings of love

Your kisses taste like rose-hip on my tongue,
our bodies, like petals, in spring's arms flung

No kiss leaves me but yearning for another;
no matter the bigotry, we have each other

Your mouth teaches me even more each day
how to live and love, unashamed to be gay

A TWENTY-FIRST CENTURY TAKE ON GREEK GODS AND EVERYDAY HEROES

Like a Greek god risen from the sea,
naked but for trunks coloured red,
he demanded I accept my sexuality

He prised loose my grip on 'morality'
to embrace erotic icons in my head,
like a Greek god risen from the sea,

Fighting nature's cause magnificently,
crossing the sand, not a word said,
he demanded I accept my sexuality

His beauty set a fever raging in me
(where sex on desire hungrily fed)
like a Greek god risen from the sea

Content to let Apollo dry his fine body,
sprawled close by on a towel bed,
he demanded I accept my sexuality

The full lips parted, oh, so invitingly
as he left, knowing I followed...
Risen like a Greek god from the sea,
he demanded I accept my sexuality

LEAVES ON THE TRACK

I first glimpsed him on a railway station,
he on one platform fretting about a late train,
me doing much the same on mine,
both of us making time for glances in the rain;
his hair was the colour of a summer storm,
eyes shining like leaves in the late afternoon,
lips as full and red as cock robin's breast
for kisses as feisty as midsummer raindrops
rehearsing a lively tune

I felt as if I'd known him all my life
though he was but a complete stranger to me;
it was like taking off in a time machine,
revisiting every lovemaking in a gay life history;
the rain turned to tears for lost loves
though its freshness on my skin so exhilarating
it took me through cruel hoops
without fear, and me a one-time victim
of its storytelling

The roar of his train raged in my ears
(the cries of thwarted lovers through centuries)
then my train arrived, screaming at me
to get real, be rational, dismiss foolish fantasies;
boarding the train, a hand on my arm
made me to turn around but I saw no one there,
only a sad, lonely, empty platform
much as a poet might describe a fairytale
stripped bare

I flung open the door and jumped down
(just seconds before your train took off with a yell)
only to be tossed on a sea of waving hands
as if I were object and subject of a witch's spell;
Ah, but I had forgotten about white magic
and how hope will always get the better of despair,
like the best poems and fairytales
conspiring to make us miss our trains,
keep us there

It didn't seem long before we caught another train,
looking forward to the time we'd be together again

MISSION IMPOSSIBLE

We were simply watching TV
and I thought little of it
as you put an arm around me
but lay my head
against you, got comfortable
till a hand tilted my chin,
launching me there and then
on Mission Impossible

I saw a passion in your eyes
I'd never see before
as your lips homed in on mine
for a first kiss,
but I wasn't sure I wanted this
so turned my head away,
even managing to splutter
I wasn't gay

Your face red with shame,
tears in your eyes
telling tales on frustrated desires
you'd kept from me;
I wasn't sure I wanted to know
about such things,
but couldn't run away, knew
I had to stay

I saw hope flare in your face
in spite of the tears;
suddenly, you had me pinioned
against a plump cushion,
my poor heart thumping madly
as your quivering lips
found their target this time
if clumsily

Your mouth on mine warmer,
sweeter than I imagined
another boy's mouth could be,
I silently confessed...to
wet dreams about you for years,
drooling over your body
in the showers after Games
or P E

The weight of your body lighter,
your kiss less determined,
I felt your confusion burning
a hole in my shirt,
struggled to reason why my mind
should resist this being kissed
that was, after all, but answering
a cry from the heart

You, now retreating, expressions
of guilt and pain
reasserting senses I'd fought
for so long to ignore,
I flung my arms around you
and pulled you close,
free at last to experience the joy
of mutual response

[Continued]

We made love on fluffy rug
(he'd brought a condom)
till all we wanted to do was stay
in each other's arms,
no more lies or even words,
just an intimate silence
saying more than even lovers
can express

[Note: Written for LGBT History Month 2011 in response to a
teenager who contacted me to say his gay relationship with a boy at
the same school had been discovered and how they had been told it
was unnatural and a sin so they could expect to go to hell for it.]

WHERE TICK-BOX CURRICULA FOUND WANTING

The first time we made love,
we were like young rabbits living in fear
of an owl swooping down

It was under a leafy awning,
in woods where we'd played as children
although never like this

As twilight cast a golden glow
across the scene, we caved in to feelings
we'd resisted for years

Oh, the bliss of physical love,
acting out its beautiful poetry, unspoken
till now but for its tears

Ah, but freedom was an illusion
if not the love consuming us that summer,
schooldays shut in a closet

Gossip raged. By the winter term,
we had gone separate ways, heads bowed,
twin hearts ripped out

To our shame, we let bigotry
get the better of us, an awakening sexuality
tempered by immaturity

Years on, mature adults now;
if a bigot's penchant for bullying still about,
more of us standing up to it

ONE KISS

One kiss, I place above all others,
conveying the passion of a midsummer night
bringing to the heart of my darkness
all the comfort and joy of an armchair firelight,
letting my natural sexuality go free,
drop all pretence of pandering to conventions
bent on persecuting me

One kiss, I place above all others,
urging me not to feel ashamed but come out
fighting (win or lose) if I must,
not for my sake but a centuries-old birthright
to wear Earth Mother's colours
with pride instead of pandering to conventions
nailing bars to my windows

One kiss, I place above all others,
treading, oh, so gently on the sweetest dreams,
flooding my body with the heat
of an insatiable spirituality tearing at its seams,
anxious to wear its colours
with pride instead of pandering to conventions
mapping out the world's scars

One kiss I place above all others
brought me to my knees as you lay me down
in the cradle of history
that has seen the same white christening gown
passed on through the ages
by those choosing not to pander to conventions,
be taken for freaks, put in cages

It's a gay kiss I place above all others, my first;
one I've since nurtured, watched grow, seen last

MILLIONS LIKE US

We took a walk beside a river,
my gay love and I,
not a care in the world
or cloud in the sky,
when they rushed out of bushes,
caught us by surprise,
calling us names, yelling lies
that have haunted
people like us for centuries

They dragged us to the ground,
beat us senseless
then ran off, laughing loudly
and telling jokes
though no one around to hear
except birds in trees
anxious to express an empathy
that has comforted
people like us for centuries

In time, we staggered to our feet
in terrible pain,
made our way to the hospital,
were patched up again
then off home, our separate ways,
as gay men did then
in those fearful, tearful days
that have haunted
people like us for centuries

It's very different now (they say);
the law's on our side,
gay men and women can raise
their hands with pride
when asked about their sexuality,
get married, even adopt,
protected from the bigot's cries
that have haunted
people like us for centuries

We took a walk beside a river
my gay love and I,
not a care in the world
or cloud in the sky,
as free as birds where humanity
killing off their trees
and nature's blessing for kisses
that have haunted
people like us for centuries

PUTTING THE WORLD TO RIGHTS

We met at a pub in Camden Town,
having arranged it all on the Internet;
at first, we weren't sure we'd like
each other and sex a blurred image
in our minds

After failing to put the world right,
we felt more at ease with each other;
I began to take in a fullness of lips,
titillated by shared if subtle intimacies
of body language

It was as if his voice lost its words
a twinkle in each eye distracting me,
several shirt buttons left undone
inviting me to appreciate dark ripples
of flesh within

By the time the conversation turned
to who should go to whose for coffee,
I had already slipped under a duvet
let him enter me, transcend the poetry
of imagination

No duvet greeted me, but satin sheets,
caressing my body even before his turn
to feel his way through dark passages
of my self, guilt blocking every attempt
to come clean

He persevered, took me to the climax
of my fears, let flow waters of the earth
succouring a lonely self, left for dead
by those insisting it's a sin for one man
to love another

If love means breaking ties that bind
generations, let's have no reservations;
love deserves better from a humanity
whose very differences that so divide us
make us human

If gay people love to be just as close
to family and old friends as anyone else,
there's a love we place even higher,
and it's a foolish person listens to those
denying us this

[Note: Camden Town is in north-west London near where I live in
Kentish Town. The Black Cap in Camden High Street is one of the
oldest and friendliest gay pubs in London if not the UK.]

SUBURBAN HERO

He was just an ordinary man, living
an ordinary life on an ordinary street,
and whenever we chanced to meet
he would always make time for a chat,
ask me (for example) did I know that
Mrs T at number ten had been ill again
with lumbago, old J at number five
caught a bug in hospital and was damn
lucky to be alive?

He was such an ordinary man, living
such an ordinary life on such a street
as you might expect to find anywhere
if you care to look beyond dull fronts
of ordinary houses, could be forgiven
for thinking no worse fate (surely?)
than this spending one's days in such
predictable ways, the stuff of suburban
myth for centuries

He was such an ordinary man, died
only a few years ago in a road accident;
no complicated will, only a pre-paid
funeral insurance, a few items to friends
and the house to an HIV-AIDS charity
that found everyone confiding how they
had suspected he was 'one of those'
but ...immaterial, and the whole street
turned out for the funeral

Such an ordinary man, nothing special,
simply a nice, neighbourly homosexual

PART FIVE

TRACKING THE TORCHBEARER

TRACKING THE TORCHBEARER

No cheers just for those who win,
everyone playing their part
in the race to show we're human

If old gods saw the Games begin
and new gods losing heart,
no cheers just for those who win,

Torch lit, and crowds making a din,
all set to make a start
in the race to show we're human

Brave new societies putting spin
on an overloaded apple cart;
no cheers just for those who win

Where old gods stir under the skin,
a new order falling apart
in the race to show we're human

Come Apollo, wearing a wry grin,
Earth Mother raising a shout;
no cheers just for those who win
in the race to show we're human

SETTING THE PACE

I am a cry in the night,
world cocking but half an ear
as it tosses and turns
its sleepy heads on damp pillows
that will need laundering
come morning if only to hide
tell-tale patches of grief,
guilt, betrayal, loss of innocence
and worse

I am tears in the rain,
no one able to tell I am crying,
no matter that I am
dying inside, needing to show
a kinder side than seen
by those who have no pity
for the likes of a cry
in the night or tears in the rain
soon forgotten

I am shadows in twilight,
precursor to darker deeds than
any God imagined
or else He (or She) would never
have laid life on me
but left me to pass like a dream
across time and space,
no cries or tears or fretting
about losing face

The faster beat of the human heart,
I give its humanity a head start

ALL THE SIGNS POINT TO HEART FAILURE

An evangelical Christian
told me I'd go to hell or worse
for being gay
if the world didn't strike first
(such is its thirst for blood)
and make me suffer for going
with my nature

A Muslim cleric
told me much the same thing
another day
upon accosting me leaving a bar
known for its gay clientele
so a worse environment by far
than any Hell

Other religious people
at school, at work, wherever,
have called me 'sinner'
for going against a God I never
believed in, choosing
to put my trust in Earth Mother
forever

One day I met a Christian
who told me it didn't matter
a jot I was gay
(even if he'd rather I wasn't)
for who was he to say
I'd go to Hell? He was certain
Jesus wouldn't

An everyday Muslim
told me much the same thing
another day
as we chatted in a bar known
for its gay clientele,
like two fallen angels doing
very well

It just goes to show,
being different isn't different,
only human,
and humanity for some people
is the heart of religion,
to be cherished come what may,
straight or gay

Let religions break free
of their prejudices and bigotry
and maybe, one day,
they will see the world as it is,
a common humanity
created for the common good
to live in peace

THE MAZE (OPEN ALL HOURS - DISABLED ACCESS - ONLY ASSISTANT DOGS ALLOWED)

Who seeks meaning, dares a maze,
its walls of evergreen
harbouring life's finer mysteries

It is a place folks fear and praise,
where ghosts often seen;
who seeks meaning, dares a maze,

See Apollo wink to shine his rays
where lovers steal unseen,
harbouring life's finer mysteries

Watch Diana's bold hunters graze
on passions dark, serene;
who seeks meaning, dares a maze

Chance on trails time artlessly lays
(true, false, in-between)
harbouring life's finer mysteries

Look out for humanity, learn ways,
to its heartland, rarely seen;
who seeks meaning, dares a maze
harbouring life's finer mysteries

EARTHQUAKE, HAITI

Devastation everywhere,
corpses left lying in the open;
Haiti, a country in despair

Little clean water to spare,
body odours sure to worsen;
devastation everywhere

Desperate for medical care,
(cuts festering, limbs broken);
Haiti, a country in despair

International aid in the air
(survivors feeling forgotten);
devastation everywhere

Richer nations, have a care
for the sheer poverty of ruin;
Haiti, a country in despair

Body and soul stripped bare,
hope slow to re-awaken,
devastation everywhere;
Haiti, a country in despair

[London: Jan 15th 2010]

This poem was written four days after a major earthquake caused
devastation to Haiti.]

FLOODS OF FEAR

Floods of fear confronting Pakistan,
indiscriminate, rich and poor;
terrorism no less a threat than rain

Now and then, the worst monsoon
breaks down the strongest door;
floods of fear confronting Pakistan

Pain and grief as the world looks on
(some say could, should do more);
terrorism no less a threat than rain

Those left homeless, no peace plan
for reconstructing their future;
floods of fear confronting Pakistan

Across the border with Afghanistan
some two-way trafficking for sure;
floods of fear confronting Pakistan

Aid on its way, can't arrive too soon;
nature wreaking sickness and more;
floods of fear confronting Pakistan;
terrorism, no less a threat than rain

[Note: Written August 4th 2010 as the worst floods for 80 years
cause devastation in Pakistan & Afghanistan.]

INDUS RISING

Swathes of the Indus rising
where homes stood, crops grew,
men, women, children dying

It's live in tents or nothing
whom the monsoon rains pursue;
swathes of the Indus rising

Millions have lost everything,
aid taking its time to filter through;
men, women, children dying

Cases of cholera spreading
like a terrorist nightmare come true;
swathes of the Indus rising

The stink of bodies floating
where nature's wrath spares but few;
men, women, children dying

Human spirit near breaking,
yet its promises to mend ringing true;
swathes of the Indus rising;
men, women, children dying

[Note: August 20th 2010. Flooding in Pakistan continues to cause the worst natural devastation ever seen in that country.]

RESILIENCE

Life and Death in a combat zone
for the lives of thirty-three men;
it was a passion for life that won

Hope and love moving things on
(against all odds, sure to win?);
Life and Death in a combat zone

Despair, the centuries-old demon
sure to stake a claim of its own;
it was a passion for life that won

Love, insisting we are not alone
in a womb-tomb of imagination;
Life and Death in a combat zone

Dark thoughts, dragging us down,
reminding us we're only human;
it was a passion for life that won

Victory! The light of a new dawn
signalling survival like a beacon;
Life and Death in a combat zone;
it was a passion for life that won

[Note: Written to celebrate the resilience of thirty-three miners in Chile trapped 700 metres underground for 69 days and rescued in October 2010.]

KIWI LICKING ITS WOUNDS

Shattered, spire of a cathedral,
victim of nature's rage,
suffering, yet stoic, its people

Ground shaking, country fearful
of its turning the next page;
shattered, spire of a cathedral

South Island left aghast, tearful
at its loss of life and damage;
suffering, yet stoic, its people

North Island painfully mindful
of its partner's courage;
shattered, spire of a cathedral

Earth bucks like a scared animal
in the face of nature's rage;
suffering, yet stoic, its people

World waits, heart sick and full,
for time to turn its next page;
shattered, spire of a cathedral;
suffering, yet stoic, its people

[London: February, 2011]

[Note: On Tuesday, Feb 22 2011, Christchurch New Zealand and its
surround were hit by a devastating shallow earthquake measuring
6.3 on the Richter scale.]

EARTH RAGE

Nature raging, run amok,
Tsunami taking its toll;
Tokyo's reeling in shock

Japan having to take stock
of losses stark and cruel;
nature raging, run amok

Ground rolling, hear it crack,
folks wrestling self-control;
Tokyo's reeling in shock

Across islands of the Pacific,
find fear draping its pall,
nature raging, run amok

As its stunned surrounds rock,
the good earth making a kill,
Tokyo's reeling in shock

Humanity taken a cruel knock,
nor all its wounds soon heal;
nature raging, run amok,
Tokyo's reeling in shock

[London; March 11th 2011]

[Note: On March 11th 2010 an earthquake measuring 9.0 on the
Richter scale struck the north-eastern coast of Japan. Although
Tokyo is some 200+ miles from the epicentre, it some suffered some
damage if incomparable with the utter devastation a Tsunami that
quickly followed left in its wake further along the coast. Shocking,
live TV coverage inspired the poem]

THE PARTISAN

I have left footprints in sand
where waves came and took them to places
they had never been;
I have left footprints in dust
where the wind came and lent them a body
that transcends endurance;
I have left footprints in grass
where rains fell to wash away the evidence
to leave everyone guessing

I have left handprints in sand
where waves came and lifted them to places
they longed to be;
I have left handprints in dust
where a south wind lent them flight on wings
of words, paint, and music;
I have left handprints in grass
where rains fell so none would know for sure
who jumped their garden fence

I have left my signature
where people came and carried me to places
they had never seen,
left it, too, on dirt tracks
where winds came and lent them brief access
to nature's finest...
whose footprints on this Earth
(before it rains) may prompt us to seek answers
to questions we've never asked

World partisan, nature's partner in crime,
I am creator and destroyer, called Time

PASSERS-BY: A COLLAGE

Time, it's passing by me,
all alone;
Stress, getting worse each day;
Love, it's all around me
closed to us...
who do not see for its tears

Society, it's hacking me
in pieces;
human remains everywhere;
Religion, it's leaving me
half dead,
trying to make sense of it all;
Politics, it's deceiving me,
so weary
of hearing lies and half lies;
Power, it's killing me,
crying out
to cloth ears for peace of mind;
Hope, it's imploring me
rise up
against the unfairness of life;
Life, should it not be teaching us
respect
for each other's differences?
Differences, once hacking
at each other,
learning the lessons of history;
History, busy reworking
ages-old myths
surrounding and dividing us;

Us, a common humanity,
world guardians,
a duty of care to generations

Time, it's passing by me,
listening out
for the timbre of its every heartbeat;
Love, it's all around,
healing us
who could not see for our tears

GHOST WRITER

You'll find me among shadows
insinuating nooks and crannies of a mind
co-writing fictions of the heart,
creating 'No Go' areas for such truths
as would make themselves known,
walk tall in sunlight, crusade with pride
against bigotry, shred it into pieces
and toss away, cocksure, no loose ends left
for tapers to mischief

I have no time for huts and hovels,
but churches, cathedrals, mosques, temples,
places where authority courts respect,
and if anyone suspect any double dealing
or duplicity, few will care to grasp
the nettle for fear its sting prove fatal
or, worse, provide propaganda
likely to earn a prime time slot on TV,
even win me converts

I always side with Law and Order,
ready to monitor and ratify any small print,
often left unread, I have to agree,
but who can blame me for a human foible
comprising aspects people prefer
to toss away, cocksure, no loose ends left
for tapers to mischief, never dreaming
their best intentions may well provide fuel
for its burning?

I prey on the goodwill of a gullible humanity,
feeding on its conscience, who am Hypocrisy

BEING HUMAN
(For Andrew and Linda)^{vii}

I come as a friend,
yet in time you will realize
I feed on
the milk of human kindness
and will drain it dry
any chance I get, even where
it leaves a trail
of hurt and pain I'll never
turn to see

I speak as a friend,
yet in time you will realize
all I say
turns on all I am, and you
count for little
alongside my needy ego;
even though
I mean no harm, I will
wear you down

I know all the excuses
that spring to mind whenever
challenged to give
thought where thought is due,
but I have little for you;
for where would that leave me
but unhappiness,
one straw less to help
keep me afloat?

I am that fair weather friend,
sure to fail you in the end

A QUESTION OF TRUST

I cherish hopes of spring,
nurture them like misty showers
encouraging flowers to grow,
buds on trees to come to blossom,
fruit or leaf, as they will
though some fall foul of a sudden
gust of wind or children
come to make sport with nature's
finer talent for creation

I sing a song of summer
though autumn leaves consigned
to compost heaps
where swallows desert the places
that gave life to their young
and the likes of me poems to pass on
though winter sure to teach
us lessons in survival even a robin
can but do its best to learn

Winter come and gone,
hopes winging on a swallow's return,
lifeless braches budding,
nature returning me, too, a life
badly bruised by winter's
show of not even caring if we last
or fade, you or I, especially
given unlooked for intervention
by forces natural or human

But let me, the dream inspiring you,
in my own way, like spring, run true

BEHIND CLOSED DOORS

I'd hear a knocking at the window,
a creaking on the stair,
but every time I looked for you,
you were never there

I'd write you unfinished love poems,
sing your praises in your ear,
but every time you looked at me,
I was never there

We'd join rambles in the countryside,
ride on dodgems at the fair,
but every time I looked for you,
you were never there

I'd bring you flowers from the garden,
we'd nurture and share,
but every time you looked at me,
I was never there

The perfect couple, we'd hear them say,
an irony I learned to bear;
whenever I looked to you for love,
you were never there

Ghosts, come alive in chance memories
of the after-dinner kind,
a template for wishful thinking
written on the wind

WOMAN IN GREEN

I sat by the sea contemplating suicide
when a woman in green came and sat by my side,
stayed quite still, didn't say a word;
my head, it rang with a gull's shrill cry
as if echoing the heart's screaming to be left to die,
no hanging on to this useless body

The woman in green didn't look at me,
but continued to exude that youth, life and beauty
I'd once loved, become my enemy;
following her gaze to a misty horizon,
I entered into a way of seeing altogether unknown
where the sea wore a green velvet gown

Grey hair streaked with a sunset's glow
above eyes as teasing a blue as those I used to know
and pink lips urging me not to follow;
where once the sea, now a patch of grass
beneath an old tree on whose leaves of painted glass
nature would work its magic for us

Vanished, just as suddenly as it came,
knowing memories will keep murmuring your name
(sea of grass, leaves of glass, the same);
suddenly, I am bursting with a desire
to live (even love?) again, like an autumn leaf on fire,
its story all but told, waiting on another

I laughed aloud, forgetting the woman in green
and turned to explain, but she had already gone

[Note: Regular bouts of depression have made me feel suicidal at
times, but I have always found hope and inspiration in nature.]

MOTHER AND CHILD

They stripped me naked,
wrapped me in a cloak of nettles,
dragged me to Hell's gate,
calling on those gathered inside
(seeking a way out)
to open up and take me in, away
from a world that such as I
dare stain with the juices of a sin
beyond redemption

Yet, the gate did not open
though their screams of abuse
did not cease
nor did those inside overtly refuse
to do their best...
for I made so bold as to call
upon Earth Mother
to rebirth me at the milky breast
of sanctuary

They slunk away like wolves
from firelight, heat and glow more
of a threat even than I;
as for those others for whom also
the gate refused to open,
they could but resume fighting
among themselves
over who was to blame this time
and in whose name

'Peace, child,' she croons reassuringly
from whom I inherit my sexual identity

THE BABYSITTER

A light shade above my head
casts a pear shaped shadow
swaying like a cradle to and fro

To and fro, a bored babysitter,
privy to an over anxious moth
seeking maternal reassurance

A door slams, rocking the cradle
as if it were a bully sneaked in
from the Outside, surprising us

Inside, we panic, the moth and I
losing our grip on the ceiling,
it flying off, leaving me to freefall

The pear follows me, catches me,
wraps me in its skin, protective
of its, oh, so vulnerable Insiders

The bully shakes a fist, frustrated
by an inability to impose its will
on either human or winged cousin

Quivering quietly, a sense of peace
ascends if lending a false sense
of security to its baby-in-the-pear

Moth glues itself to the light shade;
I, indifferently, turn the light out
and glue myself to a silken branch

THE KEEPER

I feed the fire that keeps
the light in your eyes burning brightly,
inspires the Sandman
who revisits you nightly till dawn breaks
and it's Apollo's turn
to take over the reins of inspiration
seeing us through everyday
frustration and confusion, politics
of disillusion

I am your guide, who needs
no telling which path you should take
through life though
you make one mistake after another,
even lose your true self
among its twists and turns, misleading
signs pointing this way
and that, each promising the fruits
of fulfilment

I am the ghost of lives past
calling from some distant other-world
of its own making,
anxious to be heard, reassure us
that life is for living,
each to our own, following feelings
we can't always explain,
trust the spirit of nature in whose womb
we were born

Find me, Keeper of love's eternal flame,
anxious that humanity live up to its name

THE EXECUTOR

I ensure the greater inheritance
to which humankind is born, regardless
of station in life or place in the world's
way of things that ticks away according
to how strong we are, how much
we earn or even how the heart may yearn
for a kinder way of living among its kin,
boxed up as we are, ticked off then sat on
to try and keep us down

I ensure the greater inheritance
to which humankind is born, finer spoils
of every persuasion under the sun
if it chooses to look, see, hear and, listen,
play the chameleon (as well it may)
since few people see with the inner eye,
hear with the inner ear, preoccupied
as they are with ritual and religion diverting
attention from the bigger picture

I ensure the greater inheritance
to which humankind is born whose tragedy
is a potential for greatness
beyond the riches of its sheikhs and kings,
tunnel vision of clerics insinuating
its private space, claiming Squatters Rights
should anyone try to move them on,
any appearance of mutual negotiation
but paying lip service to reason

Where its differences in peaceful co-existence,
find humankind collecting its inheritance

PART SIX

WAR, WAR, WAR

WAR, WAR, WAR
(For blog reader, Donal M, b. Dec 21-12-1970)

Great grandpa died in the First World War
alongside other brave men
who thought it was the war to end all wars,
but…it happened again

Grandpa was killed in the Second World War
alongside other brave men
who thought to win a kinder, safer, world,
but…it happened again

My father went to fight in the Falklands War
alongside other brave men;
mixed feelings about why they were there,
and…it happened again

My brother was injured in the First Gulf War
alongside other brave men
who little thought they would be coming back
to fight much the same war again

My sister is on active service in Afghanistan
alongside other men and women
for whom bravery is all but second nature,
part of a job that needs to be done

War is always in the news, its men and women
immortalised in prayer and song;
My mother always says the doves of peace
are too scared of us to stay long

NEXT OF KIN HAVE BEEN INFORMED BUT SHOULD REFRAIN FROM ASKING QUESTIONS

What do people mean when they talk about
the integrity of war?

Is it a comment on the neatness of body bags
laid out in a line?

Or maybe they are referring to injured people
rising above despair?

Can it be they mean the finer principles of war
have been upheld?

(Doesn't everyone do their best to keep friendly
fire incidents to a minimum?)

Maybe our generals court integrity for strategies
of 'win some, lose some'?

Can it be politicians promote their own integrity
to win elections?

Maybe it's all about being polite, discreet, about
to whom the spoils of war?

I asked a soldier who lost an arm and a leg in Iraq,
but he just shrugged

Maybe (the soldier said) I should ask the orphans
and widows...on both sides?

Lots of questions and not nearly enough answers
or right ones

STONE FLOWERS LAST FOREVER

On the coast of Normandy,
the last post echoes
cries of agony and ecstasy

Tear-stained faces of victory
parade in neat rows
on the coast of Normandy

Come to haunt all humanity
where freedom goes,
cries of agony and ecstasy

See the long arm of integrity
reach out to its foes
on the coast of Normandy

On the other side of memory,
pride, its dark side shows
(cries of agony and ecstasy)

For every mad run at history,
a stone flower grows;
on the coast of Normandy,
cries of agony and ecstasy

FLOTILLA OF REMEMBRANCE

To Dunkirk, the little ships did sail
for tens of thousands, backs to the sea;
an awesome task they dare not fail

Its bloody beaches saw hope prevail,
a town on fire, centre-stage for history;
to Dunkirk, the little ships did sail

Ordinary people, answering the call
to play their part for king and country;
an awesome task they dare not fail

Injured and dying due for a miracle
few could believe they would ever see;
to Dunkirk, the little ships did sail

Tens of thousands plucked from hell
under plain sail transcending the ordinary;
an awesome task they dare not fail

Soldiers of Peace, heroes one and all,
applying humanity's balm, braving its fury;
to Dunkirk, the little ships did sail,
an awesome task they dare not fail

[Note: May 27th - June 4th 1940 saw the remarkable rescue of tens of
thousands of allied troops trapped under enemy fire on the beaches
of Dunkirk. 2010 saw the 70th anniversary of this historic event.]

WAR WIDOW

A soldier's widow knelt at his grave,
their children by her side;
comrades-in-arms gathered nearby
wondering (never aloud)
whose turn next to shed tears
at whose grave?

A soldier's widow swore on his grave
to love him till the end of time,
raise their children to take great pride
in a father whose presence
felt with lasting passion nor less
for his absence

The soldier's widow took the left hand
of a thirty-something veteran
who had lost his right hand in Iraq
the first time round
before the Mandarins of Power
had second thoughts

The soldier's widow rose, took comfort
from her companion's smile
that shone like a beacon of hope
from his wheelchair
among the wreckage of a life
once thought inviolate

A war widow wipes her children's tears,
the Last Post ringing hollow in the ears

FILE ON A WAR HERO

Mind closed down for trash
like a dead Apple Mac;
any spare cash for a fall guy?

Heart closing up the wounds
on loved-ones who left;
any spare cash for a fall guy?

Close my eyes and I can see
ghosts parading the street;
any spare cash for a fall guy?

Close my ears and I can hear
folks cheering us on;
any spare cash for a fall guy?

If God's closed the file on me,
He's not the only one;
any spare cash for a fall guy?

Cops closing in to move me on
(no medals left to sell);
any spare cash for a fall guy?

Can't open up for crying inside
over pals blown apart;
any spare cash for a fall guy?

[Note: Inspired after chatting with a homeless veteran of the first Iraq war who was begging on the street, and moved on by the police soon afterwards.]

NEVER LEAVE ME

In a fairytale wood,
dwarfed by leafy towers,
we planted seeds,
watched for flowers;
none did we see
that childlike summer
you promised me a love
to last forever

You went to war
(Iraq then Afghanistan);
I found another,
my heart a safer haven;
broken promise,
a fairy tale shot dead
for a soldier, kill or else
be killed...

One night I dreamed
I ran among ruined towers
where dragons roared,
giants trampling flowers;
What of our seeds?
I had to save them or try;
nature's needs abandoned,
like love, will die

Truth to learn,
nature leaving no choice
but to return...
listen out for its voice
where leafy towers
like rousing sermons rise,
clouds rehearsing love songs
in lonely skies

All was much the same
(restored, glittering towers)
till you called my name
through late summer tears;
back to war you'll go,
yet never leave me, watching
love bloom, grow, anticipating
every homecoming

BEHIND EVERY COFFIN, ANOTHER QUESTION

We salute the fine men and women
redeployed to fight in the safer interests
of our country, those who never return
kept safe in the vaults of memory

We salute the fine men and women
redeployed to fight in the safer interests
of our country, incidents of friendly fire
tragic accidents waiting to happen

We salute the fine men and women
redeployed to fight in the safer interests
of our country, trust those who return
feel no insult added to injury...?

Who are they, the men and women
redeploying troops in the safer interests
of our country, and by what criteria
does its politics define 'safer'...?

Who are they, the men and women
redeploying troops in the safer interests
of our country to fight with shadows
not into killing by any rules ...?

Who are they, the men and women
redeploying troops in the safer interests
of our country, expressing solidarity
in newspapers, on radio and TV?

What say we to the men and women
redeployed to Afghanistan in the interest
of our country when not one politician
will tell us what's really going on?

Behind every coffin, another question

VETERAN

In the fields of Afghanistan,
a deceptively pretty sight,
witness to battles lost and won,
cheating wives, children,
family, friends, what might
have been, left with tears
of pride that can't even half fill
a bottomless well of pain

Waiting for a bus in the rain,
a deceptively pretty sight,
witness to battles lost and won
on doorsteps stretching
to Afghanistan, heads bowed
for each coffin that passes,
the soldier, the junkie, this son
or that daughter, a ghastly
parody of lambs to slaughter

I free a path through wolves,
a deceptively rare sight,
witness to battles lost and won
on longest day, longer night,
putting on a show of surviving,
giving it my best shot yet,
and though some see me at fault,
love and peace but failing,
I'm not the one up for a killing

Among veterans, all a tragedy to tell,
I, poppy, sitting pretty in your lapel

MISSING, BELIEVED KILLED

I looked up to you with love and pride
for all the fine qualities you'd nurture,
but on your last leave something died

That first time you went to war, I cried
while you but longed for adventure;
I looked up to you with love and pride

In Iraq, your worst fears chose to hide
behind finer aspects of human nature,
but on your last leave something died

In Afghanistan, you fought side by side
with the bravest, a born again warrior;
I looked up to you with love and pride

You saw friends killed or injured, tried
to see hell as part of a 'bigger picture';
but on your last leave something died

You seemed to take it all in your stride,
even carrying coffins on your shoulder;
I looked up to you with love and pride,
but on your last leave something died

[Note: Inspired by a conversation with someone whose soldier
husband had been so mentally scarred by several tours of duty that
she felt she hardly knew him any more.]

ANTHOLOGY IN SEARCH OF A TITLE

Written in blood, centuries before,
passing for a treatise on peace,
an anthology on the Poetry of War

Where warmongers strut cocksure,
find hope's desperate pleas,
written in blood, centuries before

Eyes on glory at victory's glass door,
politicians deliver fine speeches,
an anthology on the Poetry of War

Pride spilling over on the home shore
for defeating its enemies,
written in blood, centuries before

Love, waiting in the wings evermore,
can but weep at brave eulogies,
an anthology on the Poetry of War

Generations marking its pages as sure
as next autumn's leaves;
an anthology on the Poetry of War
written in blood, centuries before

EYELESS IN GAZA

Blind carnage in Gaza
(world calling for a ceasefire);
a crime against nurture

Child calls for its mother
(dead before she can get there);
blind carnage in Gaza

Each side blaming the other
(but who pays the dogs of war?);
a crime against nurture

Dispute dragging on forever,
its roots in geography and culture;
blind carnage in Gaza

Ordinary people fear
the rest of the world doesn't care;
a crime against nurture

Diplomacy holds the answer
(were politics but see its way clear);
blind carnage in Gaza,
a crime against nurture

[London: January 14th 2009]

[Note: Written while Israeli forces were conducting an offensive against Hamas in Gaza by land, sea and air as Palestinian rockets continued to hit Israel.]

IN PRAISE OF PEOPLE POWER

People Power on the street
(autocracy confronting its nemesis)
insisting its demands be met

Repressive forces hard put
to prevent Freedom finding its voice;
People Power on the street

A desire for democracy out
of hiding, staring Change in the face
insisting its demands be met

Kings, presidents...told to set
a better example, make a bold choice;
People Power on the street

Shaking off subtle and discreet,
for years put down, kept 'in its place'
insisting its demands be met

To the dead and injured, a debt
of love and peace surely setting the pace;
People Power on the street
insisting its demands be met

STORM OVER THE NILE

Cries of popular dissent
across the Land of the Pharaohs
against its president

Vultures fly, bullets spent;
where martyrs go, hope follows;
cries of popular dissent

Witness, a nation's consent
to all the human integrity throws
against its president

Above a mother's lament,
protest bursts, flowers and grows;
cries of popular dissent

Years of trial, poverty lent
a voice at last, Egypt's anger rose
against its president

No mad rush to judgement
(other than a police state allows?);
cries of popular dissent
against its president

[London, Jan 30th 2011]

[Note: In the latter days of January 2011, Egyptians demonstrated in
their thousands against President Mubarak's administration.]

153

EYE OF THE TIGER

I am who I am and all that I am
is blessed by Earth Mother;
it is she who gives you to me,
at ease with our sexuality;
no one else has the right to speak
against us who are gay;
it is her love gives you to me,
at ease with our sexuality

I am that I am and all that I am
aches for love and peace
among family, friends, a country
at ease with our sexuality
while we dry Earth Mother's tears
for a make-believe freedom
that gives me to you and you to me,
at ease with our sexuality

Where the tides of time spare none,
find history's wry comment
on freedom, bright as a tiger's eye
in the jungle of human nature,
pointing the world to a better place,
kinder of heart, fairer of face,
embracing the likes of you and me
at ease with our sexuality

There is, among all Human Rights,
one that must have priority;
taking pride in our individuality,
no matter its sexuality;
as for those who insist we deserve
punishment, even death...
find none so blind as will not see
Creation's finer symmetry

[Note: Written in response to a communication from two secretly gay Yemenis among anti-government demonstrators in Yemen, February, 2011.]

RAINING STONES

The cry goes up for deliverance,
for humanity's sake,
from a tyrant's stony arrogance

Pride plays Lord of the Dance,
(wheels of diplomacy creak);
the cry goes up for deliverance

Across Libya, thousands chance
their very lives to break
from a tyrant's stony arrogance

United Nations looks on askance
(arguing what action to take);
the cry goes up for deliverance

Dare justice make an appearance,
freedom's hold re-take
from a tyrant's stony arrogance?

Oil politics drives Europe's stance,
(U.S. up for a stake);
the cry goes up for deliverance
from a tyrant's stony arrogance

[London: March 10th 2011]

[Note: Written as civil war rages in Libya, rebels losing ground to
pro-Gadaffi forces...while the rest of the world debates whether or
not to intervene.]

HIGH TIDE IN DAMSCUS

Peaceful protesters in Syria,
meeting with violent opposition,
deserving better

Unrest flowing like the Abana,
crowds seeking greater freedom;
peaceful protesters in Syria

Spirit of human endeavour,
defying the government's position,
deserving better

Tide turning on an inferior
example of 'just' political intention;
peaceful protesters in Syria

Hear Democracy's cry, never
silenced for long by any suppression,
deserving better

Harbingers of reform, ever
brave, determined and humanitarian;
peaceful protesters in Syria,
deserving better

[London: April 30th 2010]

[Note: Peaceful demonstrations in Damascus, demanding
democratic reform, met with increasingly violent opposition from
Government forces.]

157

TERROR UNDER FIRE

Death of Terror's icon
Osama bin Laden shot dead;
alas, the Terror lives on

A compound in Pakistan
harboured Al-Qaida's head;
death of Terror's icon

A battle, not the war won
(Terror has a martyr instead);
alas, the Terror lives on

To victims of Terror's son,
hollow closure in celebration;
death of Terror's icon

Hopes for peace, an orison
on wings of a dove overhead;
alas the Terror lives on

Extremists, like carrion
circling a body all but dead;
Death of Terror's icon;
alas, the Terror lives on

[London: May 2nd 2011]

[Note: Written on the day president Obama announced the death of
terrorist leader Osama bin Laden.]

BREAD LINE UNDER FIRE

At risk, even going for bread,
lives on the line;
Yemen, busy counting its dead

Boldly its reformers tread,
their demands define;
at risk, even shopping for bread

No peace, but bullets instead,
a way of life in decline;
Yemen, busy counting its dead

Tribesmen anxious to be heard,
Human Rights refine;
at risk, even shopping for bread

Government cracking down hard
on a growing poverty line;
Yemen, busy counting its dead

Peaceful protest, by a Sheikh led,
no place in Saleh's design;
At risk, even going for bread;
Yemen, busy counting its dead

London: June 2nd 2011

A growing number of protesters are reported killed in Yemen as
peaceful protest gives way to fighting between President Abdullah
Saleh's security forces and Sheikh Sadeq al-Ahmar's tribal
coalition.

PARADISE PROFANED

Stark images of death and terror
(alien to any aspiring paradise)
stalked young people on Utoeya

A dream blasted into nightmare
in any decent person's eyes;
stark images of death and terror

Poison masquerading as a flower
(reason warped by prejudices)
stalked young people on Utoeya

Grief, disillusion and fear torture
all victims of world injustices;
stark images of death and terror

Be it son, daughter, sister, brother,
a sick inclination to terrorise
stalked young people on Utoeya

Long may a humanist ethos endure
in Norway and all democracies;
stark images of death and terror
stalked young people on Utoeya

London: July 23rd 2011

[Note: Written the day after a bomb blast in Oslo, Norway, and
related massacre of nearly 70 young people at a summer camp on
the nearby island of Utoeya by a lone gunman.,]

A CITY CALLED HAMA

Worsening violence in Syria
dead and injured toll grows;
world's critical eye on Hama

Where faith and hope endure,
to an end no one knows,
worsening violence in Syria

Freedom, bold, true, and pure,
marking up bloodied brows;
world's critical eye on Hama

Come ordinary people in fear
whose every face shows
worsening violence in Syria

Its history relating massacre
at repression's prison door,
world's critical eye on Hama

May its government yet abjure
its ways, throw open the door;
worsening violence in Syria,
world's critical eye on Hama

London: August 1st 2011

[Note: Written the day after over 100 peaceful protesters were
killed and many injured when fired upon by Government forces.
Just prior to this book going to print, the town of Homs, key to
opposition forces, is being mercilessly bombarded by the military.]

CIVILIAN CASUALTIES SIDELINED

People left homeless,
losing limbs,
civilian death toll rising,
NATO focusing
on its troop numbers

Children left orphans,
losing limbs,
dying before their time,
NATO playing
the usual blame game

Families left weeping,
losing heart,
making ends meet
as best they can,
fighting a losing battle

Media left observing
lost limbs,
civilian death toll rising,
NATO focusing
on its troop numbers

World left wondering,
why?

[Note: Written August 10th 2010. Documents recently leaked
suggest a civilian death toll in Afghanistan far greater officially
reported.]

DESPOTISM, A PLAGUE ON ALL OUR HOUSES

Indifferent to Libyans' pain,
bathing in their tears,
caught like a rat in a drain

Same old political refrain
in the world's ears,
indifferent to Libyans' pain

Lust for power in a fast lane,
chasing its tail for years,
caught like a rat in a drain

Country's loss, family's gain,
a golden gun on its fears,
indifferent to Libyans' pain

Denial, but a tick on the brain
wherever Terror appears,
caught like a rat in a drain

One last, frantic attack in vain
where Freedom dares;
indifferent to Libyans' pain,
caught like a rat in a drain

[Note: Written October 4th 2011; four days after the death of
Colonel Muammar Gadaffi in his home town of Sirte, Libya.]

WHERE 'X' MARKS THE SPOT

They called me a hero
where I fell in the heat of battle
and lay on the ground
writhing in agony alleviated only
by familiar voices
calling me back home because
it's my turn next to buy
a round at the old village pub
on the Green

The dust of centuries
choking my lungs, can scarcely
draw breath,
and my poor body pulled
in all directions...
Yet, still I can hear hop pickers
making merry in the fields
on their annual working holiday
from poverty

They call me a hero,
even those who never knew me
and will never find me
for they cannot follow (yet) among
sights, sounds and smells
keeping a promise they made me
the day I was born,
that they'd see to it I'd suffer
no lasting harm

I live, that peace we grow and die for,
at the Tomb of the Unknown Warrior

PART SEVEN

ON WITH THE MOTLEY

ON WITH THE MOTLEY

See late evening clouds billowing;
bulbous folds of a Big Top

Leafy shapes performing in trees;
trapeze artistes in sequins

Spring breeze rippling through it all;
old gods and new, laughing...

Sun's last blushes on a white dove;
paint on the face of a clown

Lovers in best complimentary seats,
enjoying candyfloss kisses

Faces shutting down for the last time,
parading out of their cages

Nature poetry, playing ringmaster
to the greatest show on earth

THE DESIGNER

I come in peace, a force for good
yet am often abused, used to make war
on lesser forces unable to resist
the strength of my will giving ambition
and determination their way;
for good or ill, time will have its say
and those, too, who endure
the wait to see if they can (ever)
put their trust in me

I bring hope where weaker forces
sure to fail, yet can be misunderstood,
seen as an enemy, threatening
to take control for my own purposes,
harbouring a secret agenda,
a measured tissue of lies and half lies
an impenetrable camouflage
for self-interest convincingly ticking
all the right boxes

I offer stability where foundations
of enterprise are in danger of collapse
along with all invested interests;
yet, I am easily distracted in playing
the hero, even persuaded
by my own convictions that any potential
for universal gain has to be better
than settling for less on the grounds
it bring happiness

I dress the bones of history with flair
who am that old chameleon, Power

THE MESSAGE

The message of Islam is peace
though some people have other ideas;
beware, who dares undermine this

it's of love the Koran teaches
though some people play on its tears;
the message of Islam is peace

To the world, its prophet reaches
though some people play on its fears;
beware, who dares undermine this

The truth about Islam is kindness,
a prophet's wisdom across centuries;
the message of Islam is peace

May religion, its martyrs embrace,
reject paltry egos poisoning its prayers;
beware, who dares undermine this

We are a common humanity, no less
for its religions and secular philosophies;
the message of Islam is peace;
beware, who dares undermine this

FOOTNOTE TO A TREATISE ON ABUSE

I am relatively new
to the world's societies
bent on testing me
to the limits of tolerance
towards a diversity
keen to embrace everyone,
regardless of sex, colour
or creed if on its divisions
determined to feed

I dare have my say
in public places, Holy Books,
political manifestos,
though adults (as a rule)
less likely to grasp
what it is I'm getting at
than a child at school
asked what he or she thinks
life is all about

I underline the words
as you read my every page,
emphasising discontent,
even rage, with the unfairness
imposed upon me
by this culture and that religion
vying for advantage
with precious little respect
for a common humanity

Abused by the politics of separatism,
I pass, ill-used, for multiculturalism

THE MAD HATTER'S TEA PARTY REVISITED

There once was a white rabbit
that ran down a hole
for fretting that the world
was in poor shape;
a little girl (with big ideas)
ran after him...
thinking it might be an adventure,
and had to be better
than moping because her daddy
had just lost his job

White Rabbit, he had contacts
in high places
whom the little girl (with big ideas)
was so thrilled to meet
and get an invite to a Tea Party
hosted by a Hatter
even madder than the rest
of the guests,
including a Queen of Hearts
and (peculiar) Minds

'Off with his head!' Queenie
kept shouting
at anyone who might have been
listening and game
to give her their vote as Hostess
with the Mostest;
she saw the little girl (with big ideas)
as the ideal candidate
to try the very humbugs she'd slaved
over a hot stove at all day

'Try these dear,' said Queenie,
'and tell me honestly
if you love them or hate them
though be sure
it's off with your head if they're not
to your liking.'
The little girl (with big ideas) insisted
she never accepted sweets
from strangers in case (who knows?)
they are poisoned

'They will probably make you ill,'
agreed the White Rabbit,
'and then you'll be in a fine pickle
with no health insurance
to pay the bills, and not a soul
giving a damn
if you take to your bed. Oh and do
have some tea,
it's a party, not a wake, leastwise
no one's dead yet...'

'Off with his head!' cried Queenie,
but the White Rabbit
laughed and said, 'You can have my head
for dessert, it's big enough
to go round, especially since all else
on offer here
is humbug, humbug, humbug - and
more humbug. Oh, and what
does Dormouse think he's doing
with that teapot anyway?

Continued...

The little girl (with big ideas) loved
every maddening minute,
was so disappointed when she woke up
to realise it was but a dream
that she pulled a white rabbit from a hat,
set it loose, made it an excuse
to chase The Dream, have a tea party
of her own, Mad Hatters invited,
she delighted to play Queen of Hearts
and (peculiar) Minds

[Written as a response to the rise of Tea Party politics in the United
States.]

I, DIARY

Sun on my face, joy in my ears,
summer jostling for pride of place
among the seasons of my life

Feel autumn drawing near,
its leaves jostling for pride of place
among the pages of my life

Tears on my face like icicles,
winter jostling for pride of place
while Earth Mother takes five

Sun on my face, joy in my ears,
springtime jostling for pride of place
among the seasons of my life

Feel summer drawing near,
its leaves jostling for pride of place
as I turn the pages of your life

End pages, no blank space,
words of love signing off our history
while Earth Mother takes five

HAIR-TRIGGER

It can drive anyone to kill,
fragile hold on life all but broken
(as if left to rage in jail)

How can even hope fill
holes in us once its icons forsaken?
It can drive anyone to kill

Actions louder than words tell
the world of a burning to get even
(as if left to rage in jail)

Where society's ways fail
to satisfy the basic human condition,
it can drive anyone to kill

Unchallenged, a native skill
to survive may erupt into persecution
(as if left to rage in jail)

Where life's a hair trigger, feel
ghost fingers tighten on our salvation;
it can drive anyone to kill
(as if left to rage in jail)

[London: Summer, 2010]

This poem was written following two separate high profile shooting
incidents involving first Derrick Byrd and then Raoul Moat in
Cumbria and Northumberland respectively.]

MANIFESTO FOR MURDER

Carnage, a Moscow Metro station
as suicide bombers strike;
when, oh, when will we ever learn?

Speculation on political intention,
the politics of blame at work;
carnage, a Moscow Metro station

Chechen rebels, focus of attention,
Muslim extremism and the like;
when, oh, when will we ever learn?

Same tit-for-tat strategies for action
in denial of mutual needs to talk;
carnage, a Moscow Metro station

Buy into a constructive contribution,
and invariably find pigs in a poke;
when, oh, when will we ever learn?

It's down to us, the ordinary person
in the street, to vote as we'd like;
carnage, a Moscow Metro station;
when, oh, when will we ever learn?

[Note: This poem was written the day after two female suicide
bombers caused carnage on the Moscow Metro, March 2010.]

LONDON'S BURNING

London's burning!
Homes, shops and cars targeted,
looters everywhere;
angry, frustrated young people,
inarticulate pain

London's burning!
Caught on TV and triggering off
copycat protest'
riots spreading to other cities,
same grievances

London's burning!
Flames fanned by social networks
and mobile phones;
street gangs feeding off criminal
masters

London's burning!
Decent young people intimidated
by peer pressure;
blinkered families, our communities
left in tears

London's burning!
What are the politicians going to do
about it?
What are parents, teachers, all of us
going to do about it?

[Written during rioting on the streets of London and other parts of
the UK in August 2011]

WHERE A MONSTER FEEDS

Eurozone, in Debt's dark lair,
struggling to reassure the world;
Europeans, fighting despair

Crisis, an ascending stair,
stability, a high risk password;
Eurozone, in Debt's dark lair

Political in-fighting clear,
Brussels, a theatre of the absurd;
Europeans, fighting despair

Its ineptitude stripped bare,
too few voices of reason heard;
Eurozone, in Debt's dark lair

Flushed out of devious cover,
MEPs, for jobs running scared;
Europeans, fighting despair

Even the Economics of Power
found wanting on Paradise Road;
Eurozone, in Debt's dark lair,
Europeans, fighting despair

[Note: Written at the height of the Eurozone Debt Crisis, November 2011]

IT'S DONE WITH MIRRORS

Looking in my mirror, all I can see
is a tear-stained face grimacing at me,
mouthing questions I can't ignore
though asked them many times before

A still, small voice demands of me
I walk tall, be confident in my sexuality,
forget compromise as a real choice,
but make a stand, give integrity a voice

I tell the mirror, 'That's all very well,
and I agree I might just as well be in hell
for this pain and fear like a fire in me,
but what will I find if I walk tall, go free?'

'What if people choose to reject me.
and I lose the love and respect of family,
friends, work colleagues, everyone…
lose face within my culture and religion?'

'What chance of getting them to see
I didn't choose my sexuality, it chose me,
and I'm the same person I was before
I chose truth, a refugee in lies no more?'

'Follow your instincts,' says the mirror,
though family, friends, creed and culture;
put love and peace to the ultimate test,
or how else can they, in you, find rest?'

'Trust me,' mouths the mirror, 'A world
for whom respect seems so shallow a word
when it comes to healing its differences
will one day need to reassess its priorities.'

Dare I do as the mirror says in good faith,
knowing I so long to go its way, take a path
pointing me plainly in the right direction,
where I follow the rhetoric of deception?

Family and friends running with each other,
dare you care enough to see-hear my mirror?

OUT OF AFRICA

'Kill the homosexuals!'
an evangelical pastor cried,
and true to his words,
many gay men and women
have since died

'Homosexuals are sinners!'
the impassioned pastor yelled
at a congregation
that took up the cry, would
see us killed

'Homosexuality is an evil,'
the demon pastor screamed,
'and no known cure
so kill, kill, or see its sinning
go unredeemed!'

'Man shall with woman lie!'
The pastor furiously exhorted
his flock to heed verses
from Leviticus, Christ's coming
conveniently aborted

Someone in the congregation
dared point out that Christ said
we should love
and help our neighbours, not
wish them dead

'Blasphemer!" the pastor cried,
near hysterically refusing to relent
his demonising
of homosexuality undermining
New Testament

Africa, Africa, what are you doing,
even listening?

[Note: In July 2010, the UK Channel 4 *Despatches* programme very
effectively highlighted the extent of the persecution of gay people in
Africa, often wholly endorsed by certain evangelical pastors. In
October the same year, Giles Muhame, controversial editor of the
Rolling Stone newspaper in Uganda, published the faces of Ugandan
gay activist David Kato (later found murdered) and other gay
Ugandan men on the front cover of the tabloid calling for them to be
hanged.]

MENTOR FOR LIFE

When hard times force an entry
at the window, sorrows beating a path
to our front door, we can call upon
some God, nature, whatever...to save us,
wring our hands in bleak despair - or
put a shoulder to time's wheel, no matter
how weakly at first, show the world
we're far from done with it yet for all
its bitter-sweet subtleties

Though ill-favoured by fortune
for now, we're far from being thrust out
of circulation as we take our turn
at the wheel, so it can be made to take
a detour in our favour, and if it seems
to have a mind of its own, so needs must
as anxiety guides its players by sun,
moon, stars, and peace candles history
has always lit for its martyrs

Time and again, we lose our way,
sight foxed by tears, other senses playing
fast and loose with a frail grip
on memories past and present, future
in freefall...till that moment sublime
when we find the strength to steer time
away from a raging Hydra
rearing its heads like ragged rocks
on a dark, indifferent sea

Brought slowly, safely into harbour
where a vaguely familiar shoreline offers
a helping hand if not sanctuary;
enough for now, for time won't be rushed,
especially once forced to compromise
after trifling so with the disaffected spirit
of a would-be loser in its favourite
game of chance designed to trick us into
losing faith in ourselves

A faith that's mentor to the human spirit
though it crew a ship of fools

A LITTLE LIGHT RAIN

The night I died, you cried over me
tears that lied, for it was never
meant to be that we'd have forever
though spring, summer, autumn,
winter years promising an eternity
of love to be tucked up in some
time capsule buried in Epping Forest
for total strangers to chance upon
in darker centuries come and gone
than knew that love once lived here,
a progressive world's brief to let it die
pick its flowers, rework its songs

It's the power of love mends fences,
heals wounds, but better, you said,
to let the dogs of war have their day,
grab a lion's share of spoils not ours,
make good the tools mercenaries leave
for other predators to fight over where
they have spilt red wine on the best
tablecloths left like out of date maps
in a White House kitchen, reflections
on a love and peace stacked up among
other dirty laundry and washing-up

Who are we to let slip an opportunity
to sit at table with kings and queens,
presidents, prime ministers, whatever
religious leaders flavour of the day,
at parties to which we're not invited
but by default, permitted to have our say
if only to seal a bargain, prove a point,
make outlaws of good people or heroes

of a portraiture long dead and gone,
unable to tell how it was, likely to go on
playing the chameleon?

Ah, I know you by your crocodile tears;
your face appears in glossy magazines
and billboards in every High Street
telling us what we should do or not do,
say or not say, eat or not eat, in case
we start to think for ourselves, even see
our spreadsheets inclined to agree
with an underlying trend of inhumanity;
Heaven forbid, anyone come to know
that wherever the lies your tears tell fall
only weeds will ever grow

It takes but a little acid rain in the eye
to blind us to hypocrisy

CARRIERS

I should have had the test,
never thought it could happen
to couples like us

Now we have to tell people
(who'll think the worst of me)
we are HIV positive

I'm just an Ordinary Joe,
struggling to pay off a mortgage
and still have a life;
I love to party (who doesn't?)
and, yes, there were a few times
I dropped my guard,
forgot low risk doesn't mean
there's no risk...

I even thought it was macho
to shrug off those scare stories
we all hear about

Drugs may control the virus,
but it's down to me we'll carry it
to our (early?) graves

GUILTY BY DEFAULT: A VATICAN DIARY

Who will praise His Holiness,
hear Earth Mother cry out in protest
for child victims of HIV-AIDS?

Let hypocrites gather *en masse*,
(keen to put their faith to a litmus test)
who will praise His Holiness

Will the Bishop of Rome confess
any blame for a kinder acolyte's unrest
for child victims of HIV-AIDS?

In the papacy, he'll surely press
the devout to place unquestioning trust;
who will praise His Holiness?

Oh, but among the lapsed, no less
anxiety to have consciences put to rest
for child victims of HIV-AIDS

Among the lasting parables of Jesus,
a Good Samaritan puts compassion first;
who will praise His Holiness
for child victims of HIV-AIDS?

[Note: Written on the occasion of Pope Benedict XVI's state visit to London, September 2010.]

WITNESS FOR THE DEFENCE

We kept our secret for years;
no one guessed we were lovers
till one day someone
walked in on us, discovered us
making love, as people do;
hours later, someone set fire
to our home, thinking
we cowered fearfully inside,
but already we had found
a place to hide, yet knew we'd be
tracked down, only a matter
of time before human decency lost
and religious bigotry won

Why should we be on the run,
who had done no harm to anyone,
lovers who just happen
to be two men, forced to live
on borrowed time in a community
corrupted by religious bigotry?
Spawn of the Devil they call us,
so-called Christians who, in their turn,
can but call on Leviticus,
conveniently forgetting how Jesus
came to bring Light,
to the world, not Terror serving
some darker power

No hungrier for power than those
who see themselves as better than us
who simply get on with our lives,
discovering in our love for each other
a dream that lasts forever;
no lonelier, in reality, than the teacher
revelling in self-delusion,
hell bent upon turning even the stuff
of religious conviction
into tragic illusion for having chosen
to side with its destruction
until a sleeplessness that lasts forever
in the grip of Earth Mother

Where sexuality on trial for causing offence,
find God, first Witness for the Defence

PERFECT STORM

Black cloud
chasing me
over blue grass and green sea;
twilight's waves
teasing me,
dumping seaweed at my feet;
a shadowy surfer
homing in on me
over weepy grass and angry sea;
I try to turn,
black cloud pinioning me
to blue grass,
a green sea clothing me
in seaweed,
shadowy surfer
skimming every nuance of mind
and body

Black cloud
imposing
a vast, appalling darkness;
twilight's waves
thundering me
for tearing at seaweed;
shadowy surfer
poised to catch me up
and drag me down
where weepy grass and angry sea
issue a challenge
to throw off the black cloud
pinioning me,
let every nuance of mind and body
scale its threat,

dismiss the surfer's shadow
and go free

Black cloud
moves on,
its vast, appalling darkness
swallowed up
by a gentler twilight
if no apology
for its thunder or waspish seaweed
making me out
to be worth no more or less
than a shadowy surfer
would have me
laid out on a sandy bed,
every nuance of mind and body
killed off
by a surge of self-pity
because I dare not tread a board
or even swim

Shadowy surfer,
exposed for a Peeping Tom moon,
challenging me
to go on home and try again
rather than let them win
who chased me like a black cloud
over blue grass
and green sea, pinioning every nuance
of mind and body
to a sandy bed with seaweed
nature never meant
to be used to dress a body
for some dark deed,
thwarted (for now at least)

Continued...

by another victory
for light over dark at the edge
of time

[London: February, 2011]

[Note: This poem was written while I was waiting for the results of
a biopsy to ascertain the nature of a large tumour in my prostate; it
confirmed I have prostate cancer albeit not aggressive. A course of
hormone therapy has since drastically reduced my PSA level so I
decided against radiotherapy if only for now...]

SOME DAYS SMACK OF BURNING RUBBER

Shadows like ghosts, burning rubber on the highway
come dead of night

One mischief-making ghost gets to play at navigator
for old times sake

Driver takes a shortcut across a field of bad dreams
sprouting like four-leaf clover

Ghosts, like shadows, ready to drive a hard bargain
with the living for their favours

Driver on a Big Wheel, screaming for the fun of a fair
under an acid rain of spreadsheets

Driver on a shrinking wheel, Gulliver lost in Lilliput
without a map

Highway coursing the driver's veins as sure as boards
turning an actor inside out

Driver's eyes opening. Wheel of Life resumes a pace
unworthy of a ghost

Home stretch, final act, driver's waking up to a kinder
endgame than limbo…?

Shadows, like ghosts, burning rubber on the highway
come dead of night

MAKING PEACE WITH MORTALITY

I saw an old man
looking in a toyshop window
just as the first snow
of winter was falling on passers-by,
and all the toys there
started singing and dancing
as if they understood
January Sales are on, someone
might buy them
for the love of a child who would
give them a home

I saw the old man
step into the toyshop window
through a curtain of snow
though winter already turning harsh
on passers-by,
and the singing-dancing toys
made him welcome,
not did it matter that he was old
and they were toys
since spreading love and peace
is down to all of us

I saw the old man
wave his hands and kick his feet,
arthritis forgotten,
keen to show he's still young at heart
and even the cruellest winter
cannot quite obliterate a spring
that will last forever
as long as one toyshop window
nurtures its seeds with pride,

recalling even the dourest cynic
to a teddy bears' picnic

His face at the window,
sight blurred, sweet-tasting tears
like rain to spring flowers,
the old man bade cheerful goodbyes
to the fun loving toys
filling the shelves, leathery face
wearing a knowing smile
acknowledging more mistakes
than a shaggy dog's hairs
and age as no more or less than
the sum of its memories

Between lines on his face
(for anyone who cared to read)
tales worth the telling,
lessons to be learned and passed on
to each girl and boy
by their favourite toy as we grow,
how though it (like us)
may fade, like the first flower
of spring, each New Year
offers us the potential to effect
repair and renewal

You'll have guessed that man was me,
making a peace of sorts with mortality

JOURNEY INTO SPACE

Stars on the water like little ships
sailing down the river;
full moon like a lighthouse beacon
guiding them to harbour;
shadows on the bank applauding
the event
like ghosts from history's pages
passing by

No one about but lovers, you and I,
keepers of the night
on behalf of all kinder humanity
while nature sleeps;
for a while, even ghosts dare relate
to the little ships
sailing past like wistful thoughts
on a leafy breeze

We pause, you and I, enjoying a rare
sense of freedom,
engaging with Earth Mother, at peace
before dawn's call to arms;
there will be other nights, ships too,
but none like this;
see the universe open up its heart
and let us in

Come night's illusions beaten to pulp
by daylight's hooves,
its lovers shall bear witness wherever
shadows gather
to empathise with time's penchant
for mortality
and nature's persistent, eternal passion
for life

LEFTOVERS

'Come into the shade,' cry ghosts
of seasons past, 'and share the feast
that lasts forever, never fear to hear
the groans of hungry men and women
or whimpering skeletons of children
reassured pain is a passport to Heaven,
all things under the sun God-given

'Come into the shade,' cry ghosts
of seasons past, 'and toast the peace
that lasts forever, never fear to hear
the groans of warring men and women
or whimpering children left to pray,
reassured price for war is paid in pain,
all things under the sun God-given

'Come into the shade,' cry ghosts
of seasons past, 'and let's play the jest
that lasts forever on those who hear
the groans of brave men and women
trying to save the planet's children,
keep its trees fairest shades of green,
feed refugees, let asylum seekers in

Feast well, ghosts, on our seasons past,
the leftovers of inhumanity sure to last

ALLY IN THE LINE OF FIRE

Where society a well-heeled liar
(politics but a blame game)
find a sharp-tongued ally in satire

They say, 'no smoke without fire'
(EEC by any other name)
where society a well-heeled liar

Odds against survival rising higher
(global warming the same);
find a sharp-tongued ally in satire

World leaders neck deep in its mire
(enjoying the perks of fame)
where society a well-heeled liar

Religion taking the AIDS toll higher
(rhetoric loud, excuses lame);
find a sharp-tongued ally in satire

Drugs and arms dealers loath to retire
(Greed, the name of the game);
where society a well-heeled liar,
find a sharp-tongued ally in satire

[Note: Humour, especially satire, should never be allowed to fall
victim to political correctness.]

CUE FOR AN OUTBREAK OF SANITY

World gone mad, what can we do?
(Rioting even in Britain...)
Up to us, that means me and you

Arab spring heading for winter too
(rioting even in Iran...)
World gone mad what can we do?

Respect for authority, manners too
(our children need to learn);
up to us, that means me and you

Where repression still running true
(will we see its bloody tide turn?)
World gone mad, what can we do?

Literacy, numeracy, failing no few
(whatever happened to Education?)
Up to us, that means me and you

Democracy gamely crawling through
where rooftop snipers at every turn;
World gone mad, what can we do...?
Up to us, that means me and you

BURY THE LEAVES, SPARE THE TREES

Splendid tree, shades
of green caught up in combat
with a rising insurgency;
patched-up leaves, shades of red
under relentless attack
by native forces

Branches, groaning
for knowing limitations placed
on input and outcome;
brave leaves, set for a showdown
with Big Combo quick to use
cloud cover

Falling leaves, piling
at the feet of parent trees
left to watch and weep;
dying leaves, preparing to treat
a sick earth perilously close
to kidney failure

Dead leaves, poultices
for wounds News editors
encouraged to gloss over;
splendid trees, pinning their hopes
on swallows returning to find
us all still standing

SPIRIT OF SILENCE

Listen out for me
a silence in the air, surpassing
all the music ever written.
Look, see how I fly the world
on wings as quick
and beautiful as anything
nature aspired for even
its favourite species between
earth and sky

Reach out, touch me,
let fumbling fingers discover
the purpose of creation.
Smell. Find in a spring shower,
urging winter to waken
where it would but sleep in
and delay things,
a fragrance of kinder truths
polluted by 'progress'

Embrace me, let your senses
open as in the womb,
recover that spiritual identity
religion so covets
that it seeks to direct and control
what it likes to call 'soul'
even if that means using threats
all the world makes under
cover of noise

Trust me, companion to conscience
who am the spirit of silence

Dear Reader,

I hope you have enjoyed at least some of the poems in this collection and will derive pleasure in exploring all seven sections. I expect to publish a final collection in 2015 to celebrate my 70th birthday. I am already working on new editions of previous collections that will be available after 2015 and will include revisions of some poems. Meanwhile, first editions are available; at a discount for my blog readers.

Contact: rogertab@aol.com with 'Poetry Reader' or 'Blog Reader' in the subject field.

Many thanks for your support and feedback,

Roger N. Taber

[i] Klaus edits *Ygdrasil,* a wonderful on-line poetry journal, to which I feel privileged to have contributed poems now and then since 2004.

[ii] Val performed as a folk singer in her younger years. We met while working for the London Borough of Camden library service. Both retired now, we have become firm friends since she was first diagnosed with breast cancer while in her early 60s.

[iii] Nuala is a friend and former colleague from the London Borough of Camden public library service; Christopher is her partner.

[iv] Jim and I were students together in Canterbury during the 1970s; he later married Colleen, another fellow student, and they continue to live there.

[v] Colleen is Jim's wife; they will have been married 35 years on April 2nd 2012.

[vi] Al-Antony (Aly) lives in Narre Warren, Victoria, Australia. We have never met, but have become good friends and exchanged lively emails since I first went on-line at home in 1997.

[vii] I knew Andrew and Linda for many years; they are shining examples of 'fair weather' friends. Most if not all of us know some; nice enough people, but thoughtless, always looking for support from friends while rarely if ever offering any in return, and have no idea of the hurt as well as frustration they inflict.